Music for Analysis

Music for Analysis

Examples from the Common Practice Period and the Twentieth Century

Thomas Benjamin   Michael Horvit   Robert Nelson

School of Music, University of Houston

HOUGHTON MIFFLIN COMPANY   BOSTON

Dallas   Geneva, Ill.   Hopewell, N.J.   Palo Alto   London

Woodcuts by Michael McCurdy

Music facsimiles:
Part I, Wolfgang Amadeus Mozart, *Rondo in D major*, K. 485. By permission of the Heineman Foundation, New York.

Part II, Frédéric Chopin, *Waltz for Piano*, op. 69, no. 1. By permission of The Garden Library, Dumbarton Oaks, Washington, D.C.

Part III, Arnold Schönberg, *Pierrot Lunaire*, "Colombine." Used by permission of Belmont Music Publishers, Los Angeles, California 90049.

Acknowledgment is made to the following sources of reprinted materials, alphabetically listed by publisher:

ASSOCIATED MUSIC PUBLISHERS, INC.
Henry Cowell, *Tiger*. Used by permission of Associated Music Publishers.

BELMONT MUSIC PUBLISHERS
Arnold Schönberg, *Piano Pieces*, op. 19, nos. 2, 4; and *Suite für Klavier*, op. 25. Used by permission of Belmont Music Publishers, Los Angeles, California 90049.

BELWIN MILLS PUBLISHING CORP.
Paul Hindemith, *Ludus Tonalis*, Fugue #2, Copyright © 1942 by B. Schott's Sohne. Copyright renewed 1970. Used by Permission. All Rights Reserved.

Paul Hindemith, *Mathis der Maler*, "Grablegung," Copyright © 1934 by B. Schott's Sohne. Copyright renewed 1962. Used by Permission. All Rights Reserved.

BOOSEY & HAWKES, INC.
Béla Bartok, *Concerto for Orchestra*. © Copyright 1946 by Hawkes and Son, London, Ltd.; Renewed 1973. Reprinted by permission of Boosey & Hawkes, Inc.

Béla Bartok, *44 Violin Duets*. © Copyright 1933 by Universal Edition, Ltd.; Renewed 1960. Copyright and Renewal assigned to Boosey & Hawkes, Inc. Reprinted by permission of Boosey & Hawkes, Inc.

Béla Bartok, *Mikrokosmos*. © Copyright 1940 by Hawkes & Son (London) Ltd.; Renewed 1967. Reprinted by permission of Boosey & Hawkes, Inc.

Béla Bartok, *String Quartet #4*. © Copyright 1929 by Universal Edition. Renewed 1956. Copyright and Renewal assigned to Boosey & Hawkes, Inc. Reprinted by permission of Boosey & Hawkes, Inc.

Benjamin Britten, *A Ceremony of Carols*. © Copyright 1943 by Boosey & Co., Ltd. Renewed 1970. Reprinted by permission of Boosey & Hawkes, Inc.

Carlisle Floyd, "The Trees on the Mountain" (*Susannah*). © Copyright 1956, 1957 by Boosey & Hawkes, Inc. Reprinted by permission of Boosey & Hawkes, Inc.

Igor Stravinsky, *Piano Sonata*. © Copyright 1925 by Edition Russe de Musique. Renewed 1952. Copyright and renewal assigned to Boosey & Hawkes, Inc. Reprinted by permission of Boosey & Hawkes, Inc.

Igor Stravinsky, *The Rake's Progress*. © Copyright 1949, 1950, 1951 by Boosey & Hawkes, Inc. Reprinted by permission of Boosey & Hawkes, Inc.

EDITIONS MAX ESCHIG
Darius Milhaud, *Saudades do Brasil*, no. 7. Pour la Grande-Bretagne et Colonies, Schott & Co., 48, Great Marlborough Street, London W.1. Pour l'Allemagne, l'Autriche, la Tchéco-Slovaquie et la Yougo-Slavie, B. Schott's Söhne, Mayence-Leipzig. Used by permission.

Francis Poulenc, *Valse*. Copyright by E. Demets 1920. Pour la Grande-Bretagne et Colonies, Schott & Co., Londres. Used by permission.

Contents

Preface

Most teachers of music theory now agree that any musical study should focus on the music itself, rather than on abstractions derived from it. We have assembled this anthology in the belief that musical anthologies provide students the most convenient access to a wide variety of music. Organized by techniques and materials, this collection features:

1. A systematic and cumulative format, organized in terms of harmonic content. The order of presentation coincides with the order both of our *Techniques and Materials of Tonal Music* and of many other music theory textbooks.

2. A compendious section devoted to twentieth-century examples, also organized systematically in terms of content. Each example has been chosen to illustrate the technique in question clearly and in an educationally efficient manner.

3. A detailed analytic checklist and sample analysis (Appendix A), provided as a guide to the student.

4. An index of composers, to facilitate study of a particular composer or style. A wide variety of textures and styles is presented; examples of chamber music, chorales, other vocal music, orchestral music in short score or reduced for piano, and keyboard music are included. Most excerpts are of at least period length, and complete short works are provided throughout. Thus this anthology can be used for courses in style, musical idiom, small forms, tonal harmony, and contemporary techniques.

5. Music playable by any competent keyboard player. Works of a virtuosic character have been avoided.

The stylistic and historical breadth, as well as the systematic format of this anthology allow it to be used in conjunction with any theory textbook concerned principally with common practice music or contemporary techniques.

All the musical examples have been chosen with care to illustrate standard usage and idiomatic procedure. In certain instances, chords appear that anticipate subsequent units; such chords are analyzed in the music. It is our feeling that the inclusion of these examples is justified by the significance of the musical device in question. Usually such chords are fully treated within one or two units.

Most examples focus clearly on one chord or technique, and the examples are cumulative. Inevitably, certain examples will suggest alternative analyses; we consider it best to allow the instructor to determine the preferred analysis.

We wish to thank the following people for their help in the preparation of this volume: Christine Womack, for manuscript preparation; Helen Garrett, for proofreading; Edward Haymes, for help with translations; and Lily Siao Owyang, Bonalyn Bricker-Smith, Charles Finley, Julius Tipton, and Mary Hansard, for their reviews of the manuscript.

T.B.

M.H.

R.N.

Suggestions to the Instructor

1. We urge the instructor to discuss all aspects of the music being analyzed — not to focus solely, for example, on harmonic content. Constant reference should be made in class discussion to such matters as motivic unity and derivation, melodic construction, counterpoint, cadence and phrase structure, texture, idiom, rhythm, and the like. An analytic checklist and sample analysis are provided in Appendix A as a guide to the teacher and a model for the student. Instructors are, of course, free to choose their own analytic approaches and terminology.

2. Such important extrinsic matters as performance practice, style, and historical context should be discussed in class. Clarification of problems of performance through analysis is often of interest to the student.

3. It is important to emphasize the organic nature of music, so as to avoid limiting class discussion to mere surface description. The interactions of line, rhythm, phrase, and harmony should be investigated. Many complete short pieces are provided throughout to allow the student some experience with formal analysis.

4. The music in this anthology can be used not only for analysis, but also for ear-training, sight-reading, score-reading, and transposition practice.

5. The instructor should insist that students listen to the assigned music before doing an analysis, and should always play the music in class both before and after discussion. We recommend the use of student performers whenever possible.

6. Users of our *Techniques and Materials of Tonal Music* (Houghton Mifflin, 1975) will note that the organization of this anthology closely parallels that of our textbook. The materials provided in Part V of *Techniques and Materials* will be particularly helpful to these instructors; pertinent units in the book include those on cadence and phrase structure, motive, sequence, melody, and small forms.

Music for Analysis

I
Diatonic Materials

1
Tonic Triad in Root Position

1. Sonatina in G major, Hob. XVI: 8

Haydn

2. Sonatina, op. 792, no. 8

Czerny

3. Leonora Overture No. 2, op. 72

Beethoven

3

4. Le Coq d'Or: Hymn to the Sun

Andantino

Rimsky-Korsakov

5. Trio, op. 70, no. 2

Allegro

Beethoven

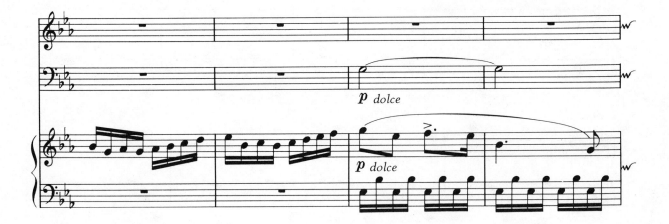

6. Valse (Posthumous)

Chopin

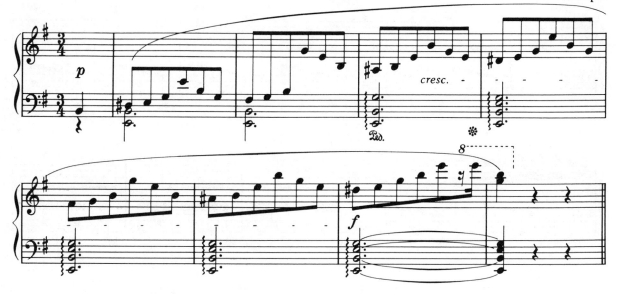

7. Symphony No. 5, op. 67

Andante con moto

Beethoven

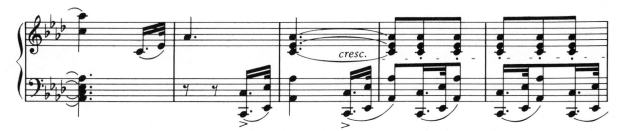

8. Carnival

Allegro

Couperin

2
Dominant Triad in Root Position

1. Rondo

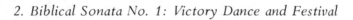

2. Biblical Sonata No. 1: Victory Dance and Festival

3. Für Elise

Poco moto

Beethoven

4. Album for the Young, op. 68: Reiterstück

Kurz und bestimmt

Schumann

5. Euryanthe, op. 81: Overture

Allegro marcato, con molto fuoco

Weber

6. Symphony No. 5, op. 67

Allegro con brio

Beethoven

9

3
Dominant Seventh and Ninth*
in Root Position

1. German Dance

Weber

2. Sonata, K. 332

Mozart

* For additional examples of the dominant ninth, see Part II, Chapter 26.

3. Wiegenlied, op. 98, no. 2

Langsam

Schubert

Schla - fe, schla - fe, hol - der, sü - ßer Kna - be,

lei - se wiegt dich dei - ner Mut - ter Hand;

4. Rigoletto, Act I, no. 2

Allegretto

Verdi

(Duke) con eleganza

Que-sta o quel - la per me pa - ri so - no a quan-

11

del mio co - re _____ l'im - pe - ro non ce - do _____

me - glio ad u - na, _____ che ad al - tra bel - tà.

5. Sonata in E major, Hob. XVI: 13

Haydn

Presto

6. Symphony No. 4, op. 60

Allegro vivace

Beethoven

sempre **f**

7. Oberon: Overture

Allegro con fuoco

Weber

8. Ländler

Schubert

9. Valses Nobles, op. 77

Schubert

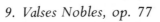

10. Valse

Mozart

$$\left[\, I\,{}_{4}^{6}\,\right]$$

15

4
Subdominant Triad in Root Position

1. Bergamasca

Scheidt

2. Faschingsschwank aus Wien, op. 26, no. 3: Scherzino

Schumann

3. *Mazurka, op. 17, no. 1*

Vivo e risoluto

Chopin

4. *Egmont Overture, op. 84*

Beethoven

Allegro

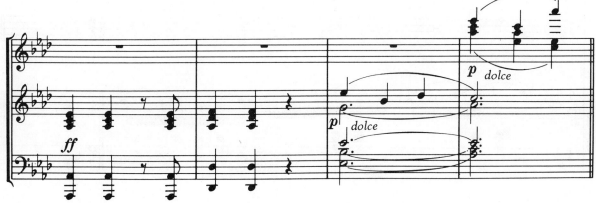

Verdi

Allegretto

Schubert

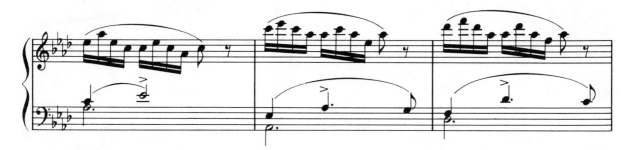

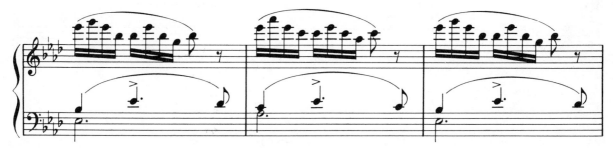

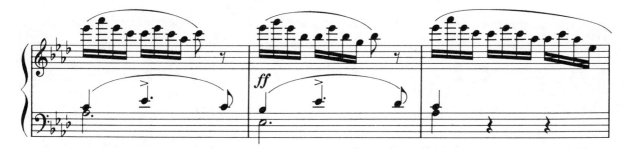

7. Seven Country Dances, no. 7

(Allegro)

Beethoven

8. Ländler

Schubert

5
Cadential Tonic Six-Four Chord

1. Valses Sentimentales, op. 50, no. 6

Schubert

2. Mazurka, op. 24, no. 3

Chopin

Moderato, con anima

Donizetti

Io son tan - to sven - tu - ra - ta,

Quel - la scu - re san - gui - no - sa

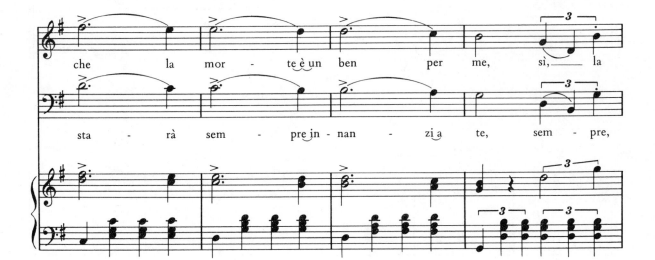

che la mor - te è un ben per me, sì, — la

sta - rà sem - pre in - nan - zi a te, sem - pre,

mor - te, sì, — la mor - te è un ben per me, sì, — la

sem - pre, sem - pre, sem - pre in - nan - zi a te, sem - pre,

22

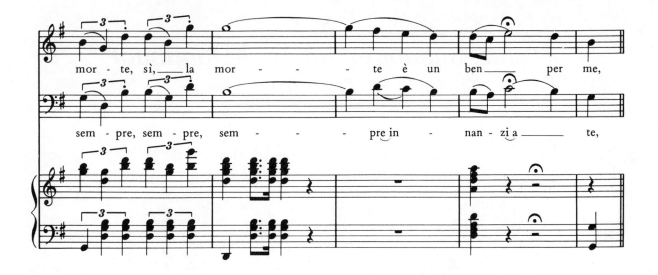

mor - te, sì, la mor - - - te è un ben per me,

sem - pre, sem - pre, sem - - - pre in - nan - zi a te,

4. Trio, op. 97

Presto

Beethoven

Violin

Cello

Presto

Piano

6
Tonic, Subdominant, and Dominant Triads in First Inversion

1. Lobt Gott, ihr Christen, allzugleich

Bach

2. Bastien und Bastienne, K. 46B, no. 9

Mozart

(Bastien)

Geh'! du sagst mir ein-e

Fa - bel;   geh'! du sagst mir ein - e   Fa - bel;   Ba - sti - en - ne

trü - get nicht Ba - sti - en - ne trü - get nicht.

---

3. Sonata, K. 332

Allegro

Mozart

---

4. Sonata in D major, Hob. XVI: 37

Presto ma non troppo

*

Haydn

*See Chapter 9.

5. Abendempfindung, K. 523

Mozart

Andante moderato

A - - bend

ist's,   die Son - ne ist   ver - schwun - - den.

6. Symphony No. 5, op. 67

Beethoven

Allegro

26

7. Sonata, K. 570

Adagio   Mozart

ii₆

8. Elijah, op. 70, no. 29

Allegro moderato   Mendelssohn

He, watch - ing Is - - - - ra - el,

He, watch - ing Is - ra - el,

He, watch- - - ing

He, watch - ing Is - ra -

slum - - - - - - - bers — not, nor sleeps.

slum - - - - - - bers not, nor sleeps.

— slum - - - - bers not, nor sleeps.

el, — slum - - bers not, nor sleeps.

9. Le Petit Rien

(Allegro)

Couperin

10. Les Fifres

Vif

Dandrieu

ii

7
Supertonic Triad

1. Dir, dir, Jehovah, will ich singen

Anon.

2. Waltz

Schubert

3. Six Variations on "Nel cor più non mi sento"

Theme

Beethoven

4. *Die Zauberflöte, K. 620, Act II, no. 21*

Mozart

Klin - get, Glöck - chen, klin - get! schafft mein Mäd - chen her,

klin - get, Glöck - chen, klin - get! bringt mein Mäd - chen her,

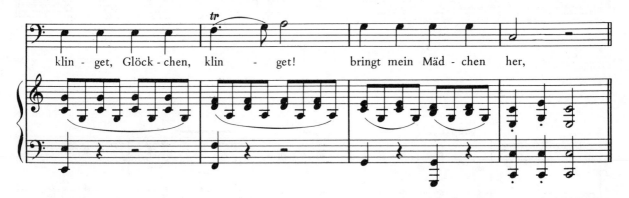

5. *Trio, op. 121A*

Beethoven

Violin

Cello

Piano

6. Rigoletto, Act III, no. 14

Verdi

Sì, ven - det - ta,___ tre-
men - - da vendet - ta di que -
st'a - - ni ma è so - - lo de - si - o.

7. Mazurka, op. 33, no. 2

Vivace

Chopin

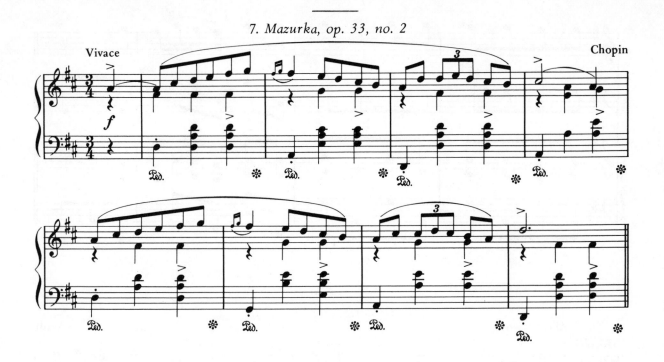

8. Sonata in E minor, Hob. XVI: 34

Adagio

Haydn

8
Inversions of the Dominant Seventh Chord

1. Nun danket alle Gott

Bach

2. Sonata in C major, Hob. XVI: 35

Haydn

Allegro

3. Le donne sur balcone

Paisiello

Le don-ne sul bal - co - ne   so be - ne in-do-vi -

nar.   I gio - va-ni al can - to - ne   so me-glio stuz-zi - car.

4. Quartet, K. 464

Mozart

34

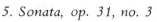

5. Sonata, op. 31, no. 3

Allegretto vivace

Beethoven

6. Trio in C major, Hob. XV: 3

Haydn*

*Possibly by Pleyel.

---

7. Sonatina, op. 20, no. 1

Allegro   Kuhlau

---

8. Symphony No. 2, op. 36

Allegro molto   Beethoven

---

9. Minuet in C

Moderato

Beethoven

* See Part I, Chapter 9.

9
Linear (Embellishing)
Six-Four Chords

---

1. Concerto No. 1 for Piano, op. 15

Beethoven

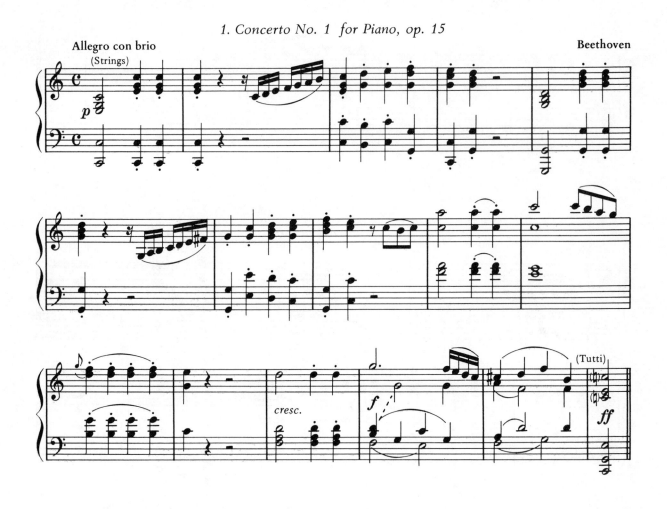

---

2. Valses Sentimentales, op. 50

Schubert

3. Rondo, K. 485

Allegro

Mozart

4. Quartet, op. 3, no. 5

Haydn

Andante cantabile

5. Waltz

Schubert

6. Symphony No. 35, K. 385

Menuetto (Trio)

Mozart

7. Sonatina in G major

Moderato

Beethoven

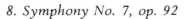

8. Symphony No. 7, op. 92

Vivace

Beethoven

9. Symphony No. 41, K. 551

Allegro vivace

Mozart

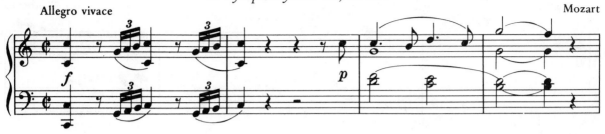

10. Sonata in D major, Hob. XVI: 37

Allegro con brio

Haydn

11. Contradanse

Allegro

Beethoven

12. Passacaglia

Buxtehude

13. Symphony No. 3, op. 55

Allegro vivace

Beethoven

14. Faust, Act I, no. 6

Tempo di valzer

Gounod

10
Submediant and Mediant Triads

1. Herzliebster Jesu, was hast du verbrochen

Crüger

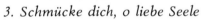

2. Dir, dir, Jehovah, will ich singen

Anon.

ii$\frac{6}{5}$

3. Schmücke dich, o liebe Seele

Bach

4. Bastien und Bastienne, K. 46B, no. 1

Andante, un poco adagio

Mozart

Mein lieb -ster Freund hat mich ver - las - sen, mit ihm ist Schlaf__ und

Ruh' da - hin, mit ihm ist Schlaf und__ Ruh' da - hin.

5. Sonata, K. 545

Rondo

Mozart

6. Sonata in F for Flute and Continuo

Allegro

Handel

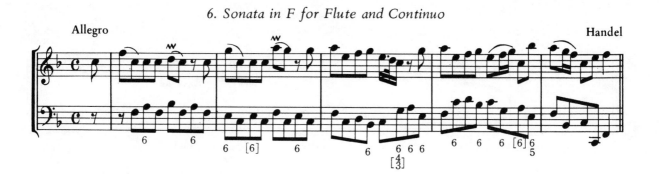

7. Rigoletto, Act I, no. 1

Allegro con brio

Verdi

8. Symphony No. 4, op. 98

Allegro giocoso

Brahms

9. Sonata for Violin and Continuo, op. 5, no. 9

Corelli

10. Quartet in D major, D. 74

Schubert

---

11. Trio, op. 1, no. 3

Beethoven

12. Sonata, K. 283

Mozart

13. Menuet

J. C. F. Bach

---

14. Au joli bois je m'en vais

Tessier

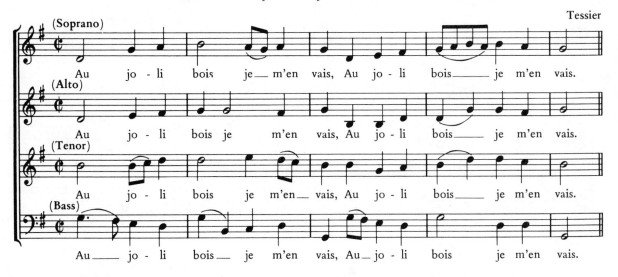

(Soprano)
Au jo - li bois je m'en vais, Au jo - li bois je m'en vais.

(Alto)
Au jo - li bois je m'en vais, Au jo - li bois je m'en vais.

(Tenor)
Au jo - li bois je m'en vais, Au jo - li bois je m'en vais.

(Bass)
Au jo - li bois je m'en vais, Au jo - li bois je m'en vais.

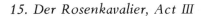

---

15. Der Rosenkavalier, Act III

Strauss

p (Sophie)
Ist ein Traum, kann nicht wirk - lich sein,

p (Octavian)
Spür' nur dich, spür' nur dich, al - lein

Ruhig gehend ♩ = 69

pp

daß wir zwei — bei - ei - nan - der sein, — bei - ei - nand' für

— und daß wir — bei - ei - nan - der sein! Geht all's sonst wie ein

al - le Zeit und E - - - - - -wig - keit.

Traum da - hin vor mei - - - - nem Sinn.

---

16. Symphony in C ("The Great")

Schubert

Andante

54

17. Romance, op. 118, no. 5

Andante   Brahms

espressivo

18. Phantasiestücke, op. 12, no. 4: Grillen

Mit humor   Schumann

19. German Dance

Schubert

20. Im Abendroth (Posthumous)

Schubert

Langsam, feierlich

con Ped.

O, wie schön ist dei - ne Welt, Va - ter, wenn sie gol - den

strah - let, wenn dein Glanz her - nie - der fällt

und den Staub mit Schim - mer ma - let;

11
Leading Tone Triad

1. Schatz über alle Schätze

Teschner

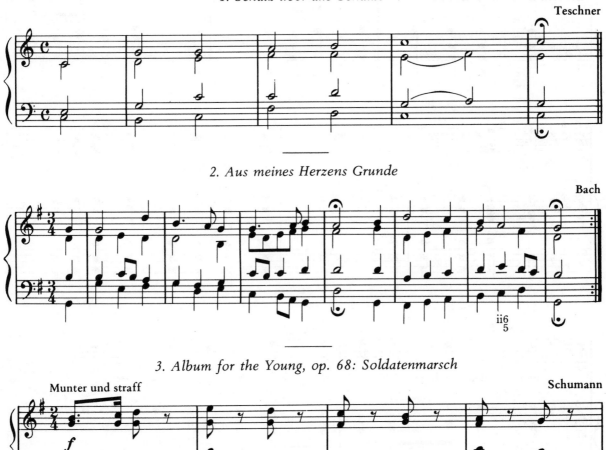

2. Aus meines Herzens Grunde

Bach

3. Album for the Young, op. 68: Soldatenmarsch

Schumann

4. Courante

Handel

5. Sonata in E♭ major, Hob. XVI: 49

Allegro   Haydn

6. Sonatina in D major, Hob. XVI: 4

Menuetto   Haydn

7. Sonata, K. 280

Mozart

12
Variant Qualities
of Diatonic Triads

SCALAR VARIANTS IN MINOR

1. Herr, ich habe mißgehandelt

Bach

ii⌀6̸5

---

2. Chaconne

Pachelbel

---

3. Fantasie

Telemann

Vivace

---

4. Pavana "The Earle of Salisbury"

Byrd

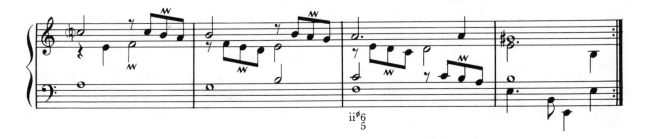

ii#6
5

---

5. Folia

A. Scarlatti

---

6. Minuet

Matthesson

---

7. Sonata, K. 310

Mozart

Presto

MODAL BORROWING

8. La Traviata, Act I, no. 2

Verdi

Di quel - l'a - mor, quel - l'a - mor —— ch'è pal - pi - to

del - l'u - ni - ver - so, del - l'u - ni - ver - so in - te - ro,

mi - ste - ri - o - so, mi - ste - ri - o - so, al - te - ro,

64

croce, cro-ce e de-li - zia, cro-ce e de-li - zia, de-li-zia al cor.

ii6
5

———

9. Linda di Chamounix, "O Luce di quest 'anima"

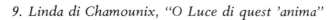

Allegretto

Donizetti

Linda

O lu-ce di quest' a - ni - ma, de-li-zia a-mor e vi - ta,

la no-stra sor-te u – ni – ta   in ter-ra in ciel sa – rà,

---

10. Sonata for Violin and Piano, K. 306

Mozart

---

11. Sonatina in C major, Hob. XVI: 7

Haydn

12. Aufenthalt

Non troppo vivace, con fuoco

Schubert

Rau - schen - der Strom, brau - sen - der Wald, star - ren - der

Fels, mein Auf - ent - halt; rau - schen - der Strom,_____

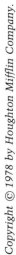

brau - sen - der Wald, ___ star - ren - der Fels, mein Auf - ent - halt.

13. Der Wanderer

Schubert

Etwas geschwinder

Wo bist du, wo bist du, mein ge - lieb - tes

Land? ge - sucht, ___ ge - ahnt, ___

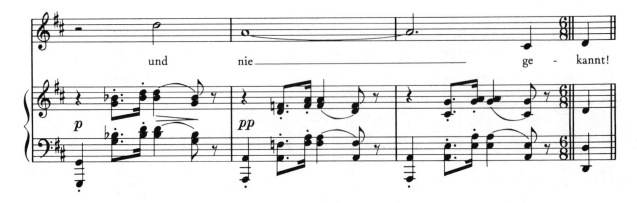

und nie ___ ge - kannt!

14. Symphony No. 3, op. 90

Andante

Brahms

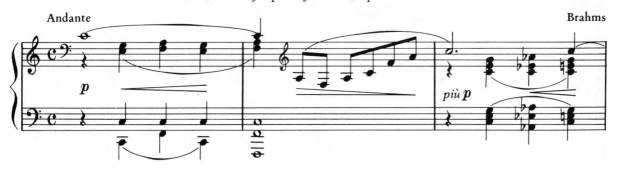

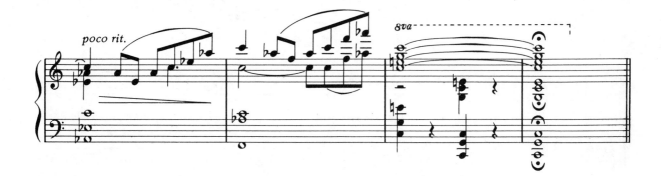

15. Il Trovatore, Act II, no. 11

Verdi

Azucena

Si - no al - l'el - sa que - sta la - ma vi - bra, im - mer - gi al - l'em - pio in

cor,_____ vi - bra, im - mer - gi al-l'em - pio in cor! Si - no al-l'el -

Manrico

Si, lo

sa que-sta la - ma, que-sta la - ma vi-bra, im-mer-gi al-l'em-pio in

giu - ro, que - sta la - ma scen - de rà_____ del - l'em-pio in

co - re, vi-bra, im-mer - gi al l'em - pio in cor!

co - re, scen-de - rà_____ del - l'em - pio in cor!

V^7_{ii}

70

16. Symphony No. 5, op. 67

Allegro

Beethoven

17. Symphony No. 4, op. 98

Andante moderato

Brahms

13
Supertonic Seventh Chord

1. Herr, wie du willst, so schick's mit mir

Anon.

2. Straf' mich nicht in deinem Zorn

Bach

3. Sonata in A♭ major, Hob. XVI: 46

Haydn

4. Voegtersang

Molto andante e semplice

Grieg

5. Symphony No. 6, op. 68

Allegretto

Beethoven

MENUETTO
Allegro

6. Quartet, op. 168 (D. 112)

Schubert

7. Sonata, K. 310

Allegro maestoso

Mozart

8. Symphony No. 2, op. 36

Larghetto

Beethoven

9. Sonata, op. 14, no. 2

Allegro

Beethoven

10. Symphony No. 6, op. 68

Beethoven

Allegro

11. Carmen, Act II: Entr'acte

Bizet

14
Leading Tone Seventh Chord

1. Sonata, K. 457

Mozart

Molto allegro

---

2. Carnaval, op. 9: Chiarina

Schumann

Passionato

---

3. Sonata for Flute and Continuo

Handel

Larghetto

---

4. Allegro

Haydn (?)

5. Trio in G major

Haydn

6. Requiem, K. 626: Offertorium

Mozart

81

a - ni-mas o — — mni-um fi - de - li-um de———— Func - to - rum.

o-mni - um fi - de — — li - um de Func - to — — rum.

a - ni-mas o — — mni-um fi - de - li-um de Func - to — — rum.

o-mni - um fi - de — — li - um de Func - to — — rum.

7. *Sonatina in G major, Hob. XVI: 11*

Haydn

Allegro

Gluck

si ton om - bre nous en - tend,_____

si ton om - bre nous en - tend,

si ton om - bre nous en - tend,_____

si ton om - bre nous en - tend,

$\dfrac{\text{vii}^{\circ}7}{\text{V}}$

9. Aria con Variazioni

Handel

10. Fantasia, l^{er} Dozzina, no. 5

Telemann

15
Other Diatonic Seventh Chords

1. O Ewigkeit, du Donnerwort

Bach

2. Rondo, K. 494

Mozart

Andante

3. Kinderstück, op. 72, no. 1

Mendelssohn

Allegro moderato

4. Fantasie

Pachelbel

5. Sonata for Flute and Continuo

Allegro

Handel

6. Menuet

Handel

7. Symphony No. 4, op. 36

Tchaikovsky

Andantino in modo di canzona

p *semplice ma grazioso*

8. French Suite in D minor

Menuet

Bach

89

16
Complete Pieces for Analysis I

1. Minuet

Beethoven

2. Dance

Schubert

3. German Dance, op. 33, no. 12

Schubert

4. Norsk

Presto marcato

Grieg

94

II
Chromatic Materials

17
Secondary (Applied, Borrowed) Dominants

---

1. Trio, op. 1, no. 1

Beethoven

---

2. Sonata, K. 281

Mozart

---

3. Impromptu, op. 142, no. 3

Schubert

---

4. Trio in D major

Haydn

5. Sonatina in G major

Beethoven

6. Oberon: Overture

Weber

Allegro con fuoco

dolce

7. Trio, op. 1, no. 1

Beethoven

8. Sonata, op. 118c: Andante

Ausdrucksvoll

Schumann

9. Symphony No. 1, op. 21

Adagio molto

Beethoven

Allegro
con brio

10. Sarabande

Handel

11. Arabeske, op. 18

Schumann

Leicht und zart

pp

cresc.

p

12. *Symphony No. 4, op. 60*

Beethoven

Adagio

13. Widmung, op. 25, no. 1

Innig, lebhaft

Schumann

Du mei-ne See - le, du mein Herz, du mei-ne

Wonn', o du mein Schmerz, du mei-ne Welt, in der ich

le - be, mein Him-mel du, da-rein ich schwe-be; o du mein

Grab, in das hin-ab ich e - wig mei-ne Kum - mer gab!

14. Symphony No. 8 ("Unfinished")

Allegro moderato

Schubert

15. Sonata, op. 118., *Puppenwiegenlied*

Schumann

Nicht schnell

16. Quintet ("Die Forelle"), op. 114 (D. 667)

Schubert

17. Quintet, op. 29

Beethoven

18. Trio, op. 11

Beethoven

* May be performed with either violin or clarinet.

19. Rigoletto, Act II, no. 7

Verdi

20. Courante

Handel

21. Sonata, op. 53

Allegro con brio

Beethoven

p dolce e molto legato

22. Symphony in C major ("The Great")

Schubert

Andante con moto

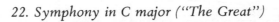

110

---

23. Trio, op. 1, no. 3

24. Mass in E♭ major: Benedictus

Andante

Schubert

Be - ne - di - ctus qui ve - nit in no - mi - ne Do - mi - ni, be -

Be - ne - di - ctus qui ve - nit in no - mi - ne Do - mi - ni, be -

-ne - di - ctus qui ve - nit in no - mi - ne Do - mi - ni,

-ne - di - ctus qui ve - nit in no - mi - ne Do - mi - ni,

Be - ne -

p

25. Midsummer Night's Dream, op. 61: Wedding March

Allegro vivace   Mendelssohn

ff

ff

26. Rigoletto, Act II, no. 14

Verdi

27. Christmas Oratorio, no. 4: Introduction

Bach

28. Sonata for Flute and Continuo

29. Mazurka, op. 67, no. 2

Cantabile

Chopin

30. Valse, op. 69, no. 1

Chopin

* See Part II, Unit 20.

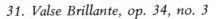

31. Valse Brillante, op. 34, no. 3

Chopin

32. Morning Prayer

Tchaikovsky

Andante

* See Part II, Unit 20.

18
Modulation to Closely Related Keys

MODULATION TO DOMINANT
1. Symphony No. 39, K. 543

ALLA TURCA *2. Sonata, K. 331*

119

3. Symphony No. 2, op. 36

Beethoven

4. Minuet

Haydn

5. Quartet, D. 173

Allegro

Schubert

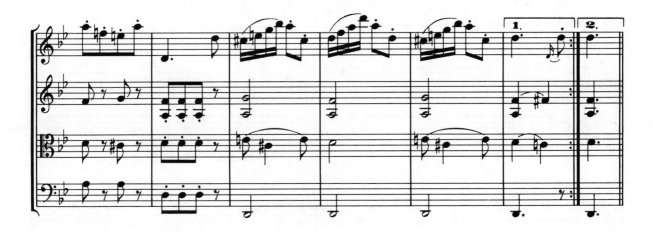

6. Sonata in C♯ minor, Hob. XVI: 36

Allegro con brio

Haydn

7. Symphony No. 41, K. 551

Mozart

Allegretto

8. Mazurka, op. 7, no. 2

Vivo, ma non troppo

Chopin

9. Sonata in G major, Hob. XVI: 39

Allegro

Haydn

123

10. Sonata, K. 282

Mozart

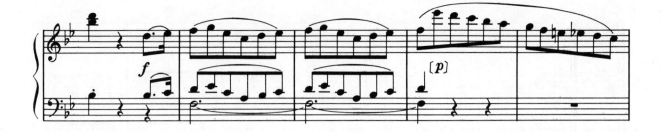

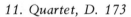

11. Quartet, D. 173

Andantino

Schubert

126

12. Trio in F♯ minor

Haydn

13. Sonata in E minor, Hob. XVI: 34

Molto vivace

Haydn

14. Sonata, K. 330

Andante cantabile

Mozart

15. Lucia di Lammermoor, Act I

Larghetto

Donizetti

vuota

Lucy p

Reg - na - va nel ___ si - len - zi - o

al - ta la not - te e bru ___ na col - pìa la fron - te un

pal - li - do rag - gio di te - tra lu ___ na

16. Quintet, op. 115

Brahms

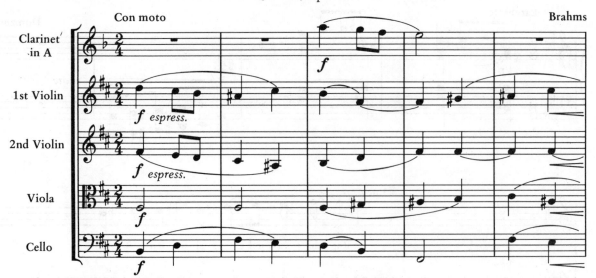

17. Symphony No. 7, op. 92

Beethoven

18. Symphony No. 104, Hob. I: 104

Haydn

MODULATION TO OTHER CLOSELY RELATED KEYS
19. Sonatina, Hob. XVI: 1

Haydn

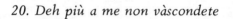

20. Deh più a me non vàscondete

Bononcini

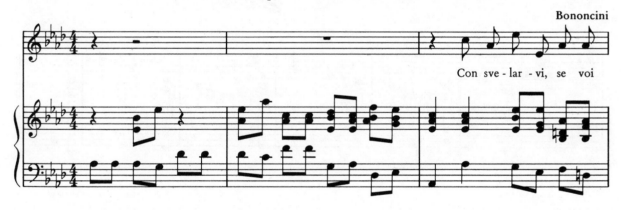

Con sve - lar - vi, se voi

sie - te, voi po - te - te far que - st'al - ma fuor di duol, voi po -

te - te far que-st'al-ma — fuor di duol, _____ far que-st'al-ma — fuor di — duol.

21. Song, op. 55, no. 5

MacDowell

Cheerily

pp *f*

rit. - - - - -

pp *pp*

22. Carneval des Animaux: Le Cygne

Saint-Saëns

---

23. Waltz, op. 39, no. 15

Brahms

24. Carmen, Act I, no. 7

Ma mè - re je la vois! —— Oui, je re - vois —— mon vil -
la - ge! Ô sou-ve - nirs —— d'au-tre-fois, —— doux sou-ve - nirs du pa - ys!

G: IV₆
b: N₆

25. Quartet, op. 18, no. 2

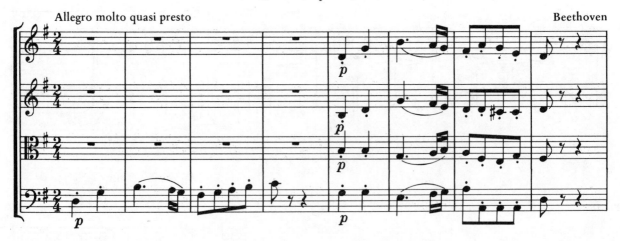

138

26. Dido and Aeneas

Purcell

Banish sorrow, banish care, Grief should ne'er ap-proach the fair,

Banish sorrow, banish care, Grief should ne'er ap-proach the

Banish sorrow, banish care, Grief should ne'er ap-proach the

Banish sorrow, banish care, Grief should ne'er ap-proach the

fair, Banish sorrow, banish care, Grief should ne'er ap-proach, should ne'er ap-

fair, Banish, banish, care, banish sorrow, Grief should ne'er, should ne'er ap-

fair, Banish sorrow, banish, banish care, Grief should ne'er ap-proach, should ne'er ap-

fair, Banish sorrow, banish, banish care, Grief should ne'er ap-

proach the fair, grief _____ should ne'er ap-proach the fair.

proach the fair, grief should ne'er, should ne'er ap - proach the fair.

proach the fair, grief should ne'er, should ne'er ap - proach the fair.

proach the fair, _____ grief _____ should ne'er ap - proach the fair.

27. French Suite in C minor

Menuet   Bach

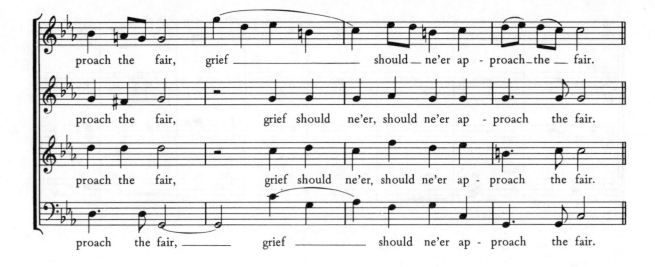

141

19
Complete Pieces for Analysis II

1. Wachet auf, ruft uns die Stimme

Bach

2. In dulci jubilo

Bach

143

3. Christ lag in Todesbanden

Bach

4. Menuet

Handel

5. Sonata, op. 26

Beethoven

Andante

6. Sonata, op. 118♭: Abendlied

7. Schneeglöckchen, op. 79, no. 29

Nicht schnell   p   Schumann

Der Schnee, der ge - stern noch in Flöck - chen

vom Him - mel fiel, hängt — nun ge - ron - nen heut als

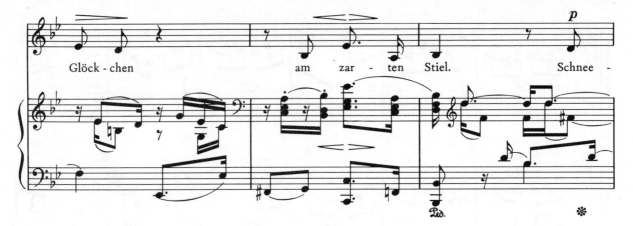

Glöck - chen am zar - ten Stiel. Schnee -

glöck - chen läu - tet; was be - deu - tet's im stil - len

Hain? O komm ge - schwind! Im Hai - ne läu - tet's

den Früh - ling ein. O kommt, ihr Blät - ter, Blüt und

Blu - me,   die ihr noch träumt,   all zu des

Früh - lings Hei - lig - tu - me!   kommt un - ge - säumt!

8. Prelude

Allegro   Handel

9. Sonatina in F major

Allegro assai

Beethoven

10. Sonata in G major, Hob. XVI: 27

Haydn

Menuet

153

It.ø

Menuet da Capo

20
Linear (Embellishing)
Diminished Seventh Chords

1. Symphony No. 104, Hob. I: 104

2. Symphony No. 7, op. 92

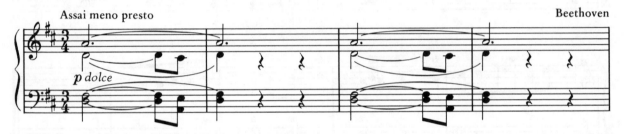

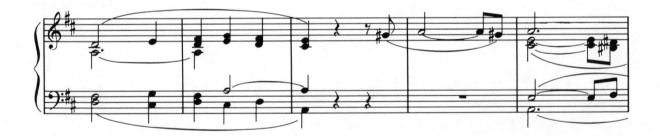

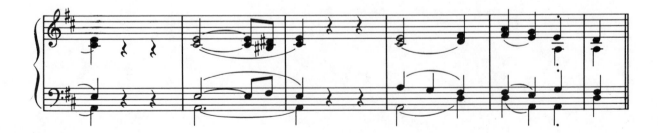

Allegretto pastorale
dolce espressivo

Liszt

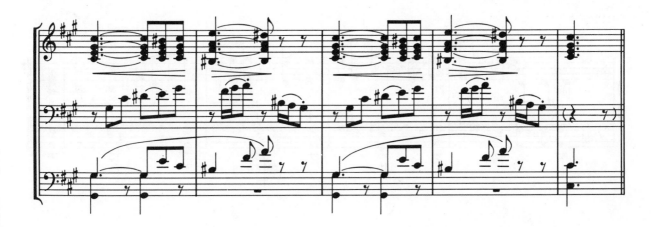

157

4. Contradanse

Beethoven

5. Symphony No. 6, op. 74

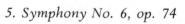

Andante

Tchaikovsky

6. Quartet, op. 18, no. 3

Andante con moto

Beethoven

7. Sonata, op. 53

Con moto

Schubert

8. Faust, Act V, no. 18

Gounod

Allegro moderato

Faust: Doux nec - tar, dans ton i - vres - se Tiens mon coeur en-se - ve -

Soprano: Ô __ doux __ nec-

li, Qu'un bai - ser de feu ca - res - se Jus-qu'au jour mon front __ pâ - li.

tar!

Ô doux __ nec - tar!

9. Carnaval, op. 9: Arlequin

Vivo

Schumann

160

10. Waltz, K. 567

Allegretto

Mozart

11. Rienzi: Overture

Molto più stretto

Wagner

12. I Puritani, Act II

Bellini

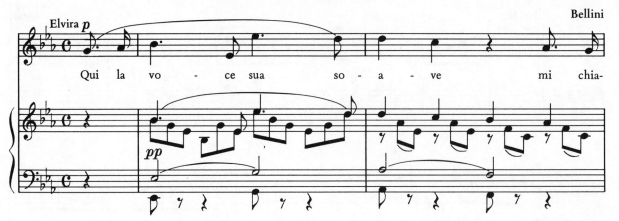

Qui la vo - ce sua so - a - ve mi chia-

ma - va e poi spa - rì.___ Qui giu - ra - va es - ser fe-

de - le, qui il giu - ra - va, qui il giu - ra - va, e poi cru-

de - le, poi cru - de - le ei mi___ fug - gi.

162

13. Symphony No. 104, Hob. I: 104

Haydn

14. Liebeslieder Walzer, op. 52, no. 4

Brahms

Wie des A - bends schö - ne Rö - te

möcht' ich ar - me Dir - ne glüh'n, glüh'n,

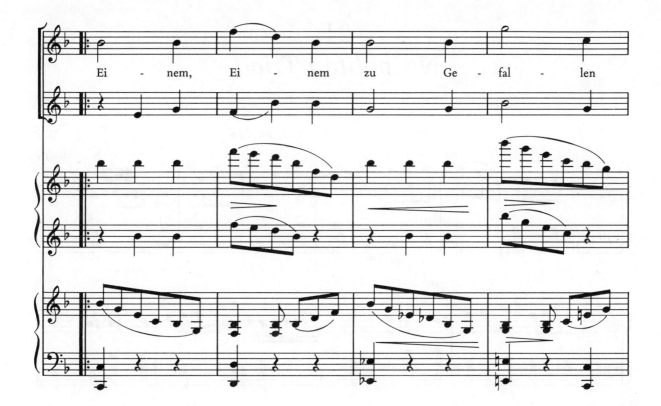

Ei - nem, Ei - nem zu Ge - fal - len

son - der En - de Won - ne sprüh'n.   sprüh'n.

21
Neapolitan Triad

1. Concerto in A major, K. 488

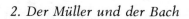

2. Der Müller und der Bach

Wo ein treu-es Her - ze in Lie - be ver - geht, da

3. Ach Gott, vom Himmel sieh' darein

Bach

4. Invention No. 13

Bach

5. Il Trovatore, Act II, no. 8

Verdi

Si - ni - stra splen - - de sui

vol - ti or - ri - - bi - li la te - tra fiam -

ma che s'al - za, che s'al - za al ciel,

che s'al za al ciel!

6. Intermezzo in A major, op. 118, no. 2

Brahms

7. Prelude, op. 28, no. 20

Chopin

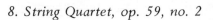

8. String Quartet, op. 59, no. 2

Beethoven

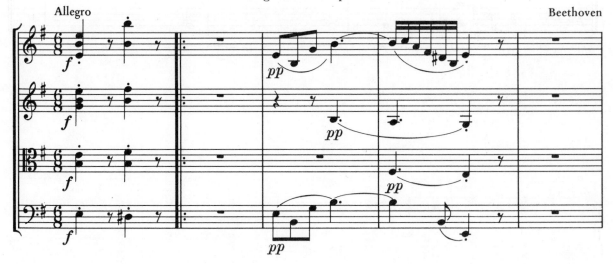

9. Wie Melodien zieht es mir, op. 105

Zart

Brahms

Wie Me - lo - di - en ____ zieht es mir lei - se durch den

Sinn, wie Früh - lings-blu - men blüht es und schwebt wie Duft da - hin.

p sempre dolce

10. Quartet, op. 18, no. 3

Allegro

Beethoven

Schubert

cto - - rem coe - li et ter - - rae,

cto - rem coe - li et ter - - rae,

---

12. Prelude, op. 28, no. 6

Chopin

Lento assai

p *sotto voce*

22
Augmented Sixth Chords,
Submediant Degree as Lowest Note

ITALIAN

1. Ich hab' mein' Sach' Gott heimgestellt

Bach

2. Bagatelle, op. 119, no. 1

Beethoven

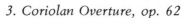

3. Coriolan Overture, op. 62

Allegro con brio

Beethoven

---

4. Mazurka

Tempo di mazurka

Tchaikovsky

---

5. Quartet, op. 168 (D. 112)

Presto

Schubert

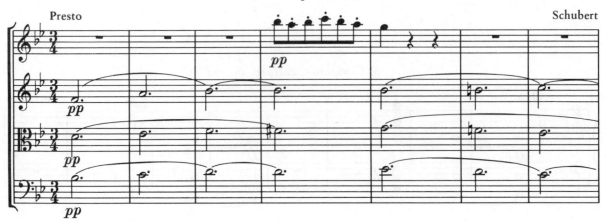

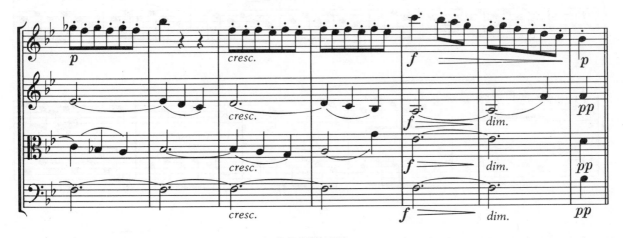

6. *Symphony No. 1, op. 21*

Beethoven

179

GERMAN

7. Sonata, K. 457

Molto allegro   Mozart

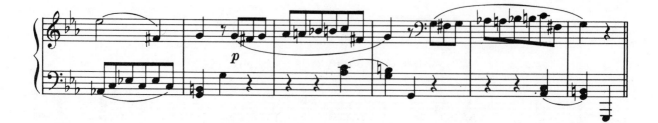

8. Sonata, op. 109

Andante molto cantabile ed espressivo

mezza voce

Beethoven

crescendo *p*

cresc. - - - *sf* *mezza voce*

9. Trio

Andante

Haydn

Violin

mf

Cello

mf

Andante

Piano

mf

---

10. 32 Variations

Sostenuto   Beethoven

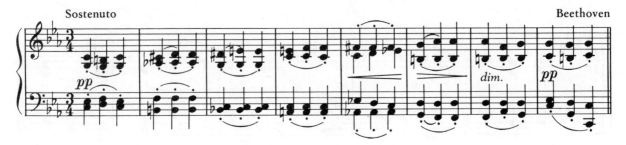

---

11. Chanson Sans Paroles, op. 40, no. 2

Andantino   Sibelius

12. Der Rosenkavalier, Act I

Strauss

Tenor

Di ri - go - ri ar - ma - to il se - no Con - tro a - mor mi ri - bel - lai, ___ Ma fui ___ vin - to in un ba - le - no ___ In ma - rar du - e va - ghi rai. ___ Ma fui ___ vin - to in un ba - le - no ahi! ___ In mi - rar du - e va - ghi rai.

183

13. Elijah, op. 70, no. 1

Mendelssohn

14. Mass in G major: Kyrie

Andante con moto

Schubert

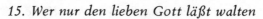

15. Wer nur den lieben Gott läßt walten

Bach

16. Sonata, op. 42

Schubert

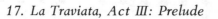

17. La Traviata, Act III: Prelude

Verdi

18. Symphony in C ("The Great")

Schubert

Andante con moto

19. Alfedans

Grieg

Molto allegro e sempre staccato

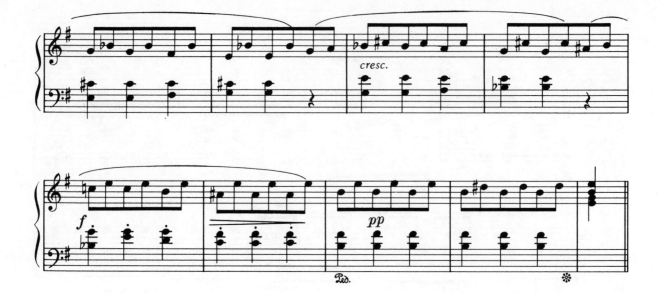

ENHARMONIC GERMAN

20. Dichterliebe, op. 48, no. 12: "Am leuchtenden Sommermorgen"

um.   Es   flü - stern und spre - chen die

Blu - men,   ich a - ber wand - le stumm.

23
Augmented Sixth Chords,
Other Scale Degrees as Lowest Note

1. Adagio

Mozart (?)

2. Valses Poeticos

Moderato

Granados

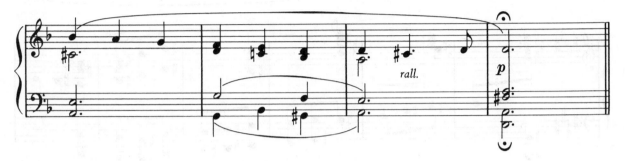

3. Symphony No. 8 ("Unfinished")

Schubert

Andante con moto

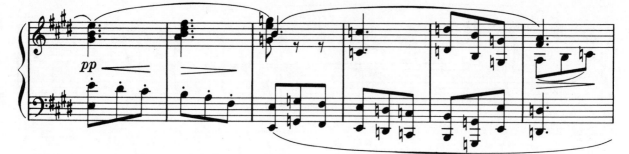

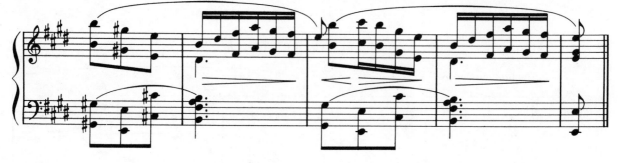

4. *Songs and Dances of Death, no. 4*

Moussorgsky

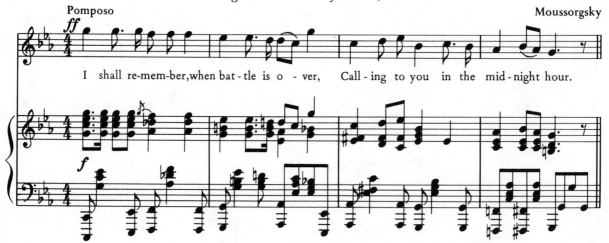

I shall re-mem-ber, when bat-tle is o-ver, Call-ing to you in the mid-night hour.

5. Orphée, Act I, nos. 6 and 7

Gluck

Ob - jet de mon a - - mour,

24
Augmented Sixth Chords, Other Uses

LINEAR

1. Rigoletto, Act I: Prelude

2. Song Without Words

---

3. Romeo and Juliet

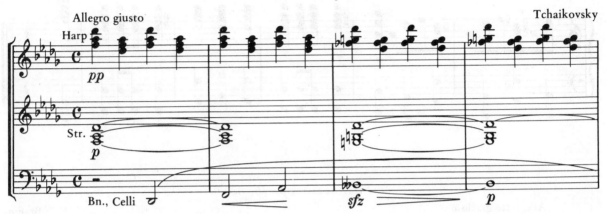

4. Waltz

Schubert

5. Intermezzo, op. 76, no. 4

Allegretto grazioso

Brahms

6. The Witch

Allegro molto

Tchaikovsky

SECONDARY

7. Prelude, op. 28, no. 22

Chopin

Molto agitato

8. Mass in G: Benedictus

Schubert

Andante grazioso

Soprano solo

Be - ne - di - - ctus qui

venit in no-mi-ne Do-mi-ni, be - ne -

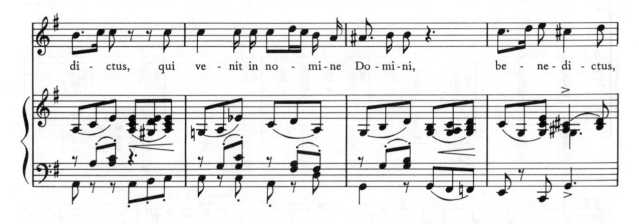

di - ctus, qui ve - nit in no - mi-ne Do-mi-ni, be - ne-di - ctus,

be - ne-di - ctus qui ve - nit in___ no - mi-ne Do - mi - ni,

qui ___ ve - nit in ___ no - mi-ne Do - mi - ni.

9. Die Allmacht, op. 79, no. 2

Langsam, feierlich

Schubert

Gross ist Je - ho - va der Herr, _____ denn Him - mel und

Er - de ver - kün - den sei - ne Macht.

200

ALTERED DOMINANTS

10. Quintet, op. 163

Schubert

11. Liebestraum, no. 3

Poco allegro, con affetto

Liszt

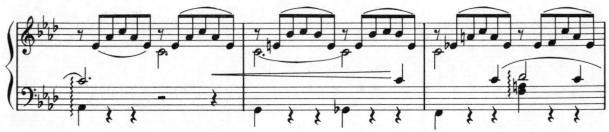

12. Snowmaiden: Chanson du Bonhomme Hiver

Poco animato

Rimsky-Korsakov

---

13. Solvejg's Lied

Grieg

25
Other Means of Modulation

1. Mass in G: Agnus Dei

Schubert

De - i,

tol - lis pec-ca - ta mun - di,

mi - se-re - re no - bis,

mi - se-re, mi - se - re no - bis,

mi - se-re, mi - se - re no - bis,

mi - se - re - re no - bis,

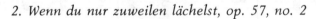

2. Wenn du nur zuweilen lächelst, op. 57, no. 2

Poco andante

Brahms

Wenn du nur zu - wei - len lä - chelst,

nur___ zu - wei - len Küh - le fä - chelst

die - ser un - ge-mess - nen Glut, die - ser un - ge - mess - - nen Glut.

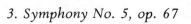

3. Symphony No. 5, op. 67

Beethoven

Andante con moto

4. Waltz

Schubert

5. Die Entführung aus dem Serail, K. 384, Act III, no. 18

Allegretto

Mozart

Pedrillo

In Moh - ren - land ge - fan - gen war _____ ein

Mä - del hübsch und fein, sah roth und weiss, war schwarz von

Haar, seufzt' Tag und Nacht und wein - te gar, wollt'

gern er - lö - set sein, wollt' gern er - lö - set

sein.

6. Symphony No. 2, op. 61

Allegro vivace

Schumann

7. Symphony No. 7, op. 92

Allegretto

Beethoven

8. *String Quartet, op. 76, no. 6*

Haydn

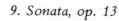

9. Sonata, op. 13

Beethoven

Grave

Allegro molto e con brio

10. Trio, op. 70, no. 1

Beethoven

Presto

Presto

11. Prelude, op. 13, no. 3

Scriabin

213

12. Die Fledermaus: Overture

J. Strauss

13. Wie bist du meine Königen, op. 32, no. 9

Brahms

Adagio

Durch to - te Wü - sten wan-dle hin, und grü - ne

Schat - ten brei-ten sich,___ ob fürch-ter - li - che Schwü-le

dort ohn___ En - de brü - te,

won - ne - voll, won - ne, won - ne

voll.

p espress.

14. *Mass in A♭: Agnus Dei*

Adagio

Schubert

pp

Solo

A - gnus De - i, a - gnus De - i,

Solo

A - gnus De - - - i,

Solo

A - gnus De - - - i,

Solo

A - gnus De - i,

mi - se - re - re no - - - - - bis.

mi - se - re - re no - - - - - bis.

mi - se - re - re no - - - - - bis.

mi - se - re - re no - - - - - bis.

15. Trio, op. 11

Adagio

Beethoven

Violin*

Clarinet in B♭*

Cello

Piano

* Violin and clarinet are alternate parts.

16. Melodie, op. 3, no. 3

Adagio sostenuto

Rachmaninoff

17. Symphony No. 8 ("Unfinished")

Schubert

26
Ninth Chords

DOMINANT NINTHS

1. Artist's Life Waltzes, op. 316, no. 3

Strauss

---

2. Sonata for Violin and Piano

Franck

Allegretto ben moderato

molto dolce

pp

3. *Andante*

Beethoven

p

mf

4. Valse Brillante, op. 34, no. 1

Chopin

5. Waldesgespräch, op. 39, no. 3

Schumann

Ziemlich rasch

Es ist schon spät,___ es ist schon kalt,___ was reit'st du ein - sam durch den Wald? Der wald_ ist lang, du bist_ al - lein, du schö- ne Braut, ich füh'r dich heim,

6. Prelude, op. 28, no. 15

Sostenuto

Chopin

SECONDARY DOMINANT NINTHS

7. *St. Matthew Passion, no. 78*

Bach

8. *Genoveva, op. 81: Overture*

Schumann

9. Grandmother's Minuet, op. 68, no. 2

Allegretto grazioso e leggierissimo

Grieg

10. Kinderscenen, op. 15, no. 7: Träumerei

Moderato

Schumann

NONDOMINANT NINTHS

11. Wedding Day at Troldhaugen, op. 65, no. 6

Tempo di marcia

Grieg

12. Midsummer Nights Dream, op. 21: Overture

Allegro di molto

Mendelssohn

13. Après un Rêve

Andantino

Fauré

Tu m'ap - pe - lais et je quit - tais la ter - re

Pour m'en-fuir a - vec toi vers la lu - miè - - re,

231

Les cieux___ pour___ nous___ entr' ouv - raient leurs nu – es, splen -

cresc. poco a poco

deurs___ in - con - nu – es lu – eurs di - vi - nes en - tre - vu – es.

27
Extended Linear Usages

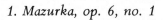

1. Mazurka, op. 6, no. 1

Chopin

2. Der Tod, "Das ist die kühle Nacht," op. 96, no. 1

Sehr langsam

Brahms

Der Tod, das ist die küh - le Nacht, das Le - ben

ist der schwü - le Tag. Es dun - kelt schon,

mich schlä - fert, der Tag _____ hat mich müd' ge - macht.

3. Euryanthe: Overture

Largo

Weber

234

4. Quartet, op. 59, no. 3

Beethoven

Andante con moto

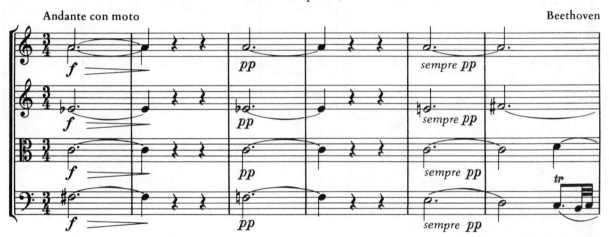

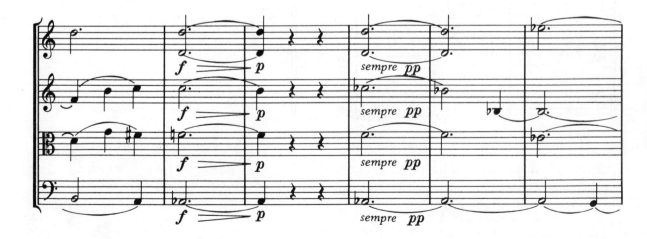

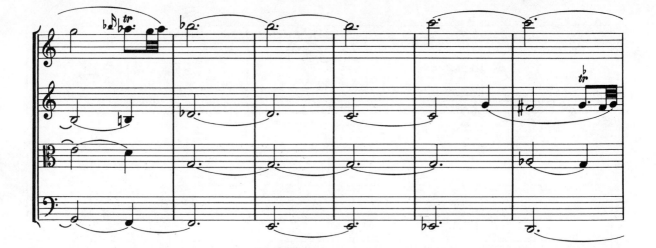

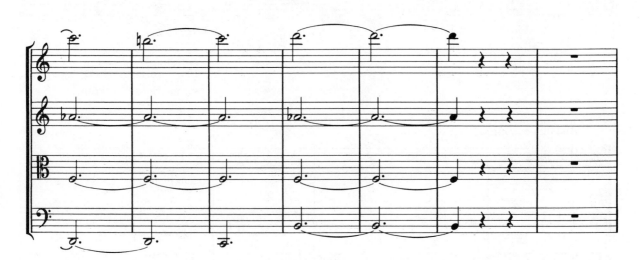

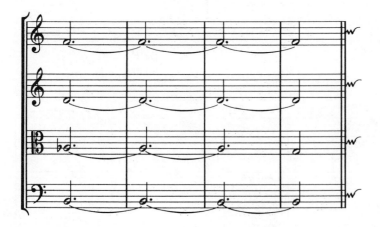

5. Variations on a Theme by Handel

Brahms

6. Symphony in D minor

Allegro non troppo

Franck

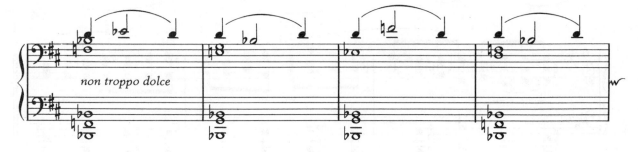

7. Prelude, op. 28, no. 9

LA MALINCONIA
Questo pezzo si deve trattare colla più gran delicatezza.

8. Quartet, op. 18, no. 6

Beethoven

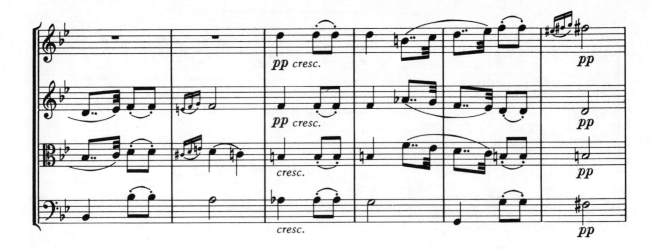

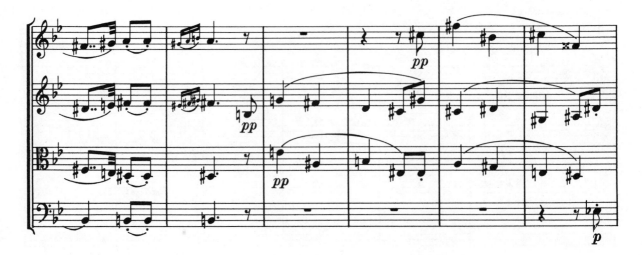

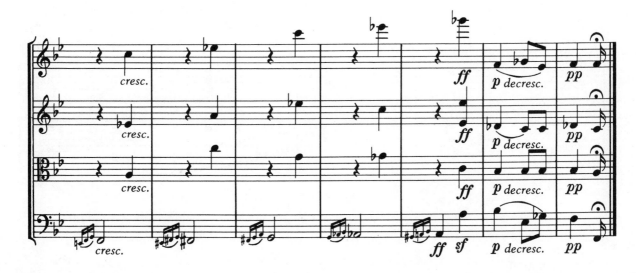

241

28
Complete Pieces for Analysis III
---

1. Ein' feste Burg ist unser Gott

Bach

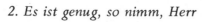

2. Es ist genug, so nimm, Herr

Bach

3. *Cantata No. 4: Sinfonia*

Bach

4. Minuet, K. 355

Mozart

5. Lieder ohne Wörte, op. 30, no. 3

Adagio non troppo

Mendelssohn

6. Die Lotosblume, op. 25, no. 7

sich vor der Son - ne Pracht, und mit ge - senk - tem

Haup - te er - war - tet sie träu - mend die Nacht. Der

Mond, der ist___ ihr Buh - le, er weckt sie mit sei - nem

Licht, und ihm ent - schlei - ert sie freund - lich ihr

nach und nach

from - mes Blu - men-ge - sicht. Sie blüht und glüht und

schneller

leuch - tet, und star - ret stumm in die Höh',_____ sie

ritard. **p**

duf - tet und wei - net und zit - tert vor Lie - be und Lie - bes -

ritard.

weh, vor Lie - be und Lie - bes - weh.

7. *Phantasiestücke, op. 12, no. 3: Warum?*

Langsam und zart

Schumann

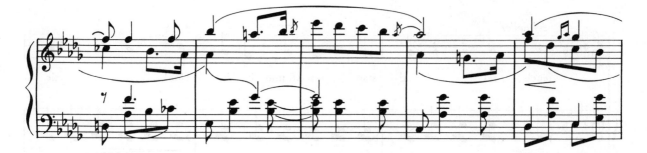

8. Erotikon

Grieg

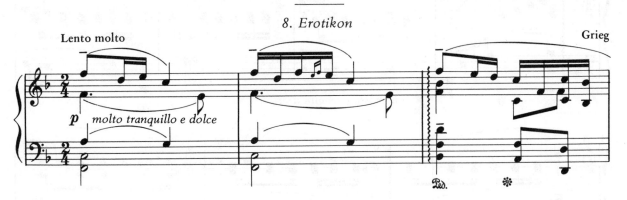

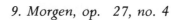

9. Morgen, op. 27, no. 4

R. Strauss

Und mor-gen wird die Son - ne wie - - der schei - nen, und auf dem

We - ge, den ich ge - hen wer - de, wird uns, die Glück - li - chen,

sie wie - der ei - nen in - mit - ten die - ser son - nen - at - men - den

Er - de, und zu dem Strand, dem wei - ten wo - gen-

blau - en, wer-den wir still und lang - sam nie - der - stei - gen,

stumm ___ wer-den wir uns in die Au - gen schau - en,

und auf uns sinkt des Glü - ckes stum-mes Schwei - gen.

III
Twentieth-Century Materials

29
Diatonic (Church) Modes

1. Little Pieces for Children, no. III

2. Ten Preludes, no. I

Andantino espressivo ♩ = 84

Chávez

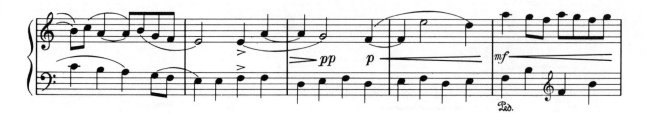

3. Valse

Assez vif

Poulenc

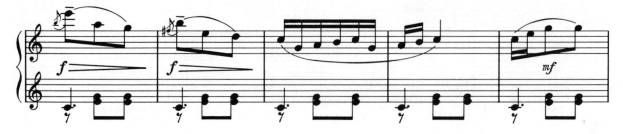

mf cinglez les, appogiatures

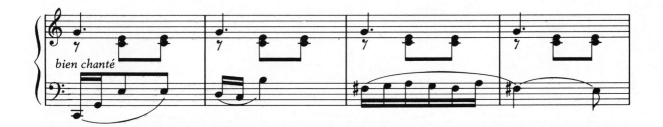

bien chanté

4. Trois Chansons, no. I

Très modéré, soutenu et expressif

Debussy

Dieu! qu'il la fait bon re - gar - der La gra - ci - eu - se bonne et

bel - le;

5. Toccatina

Allegretto

Kabalevsky

6. Ceremony of Carols, no. 8

Britten

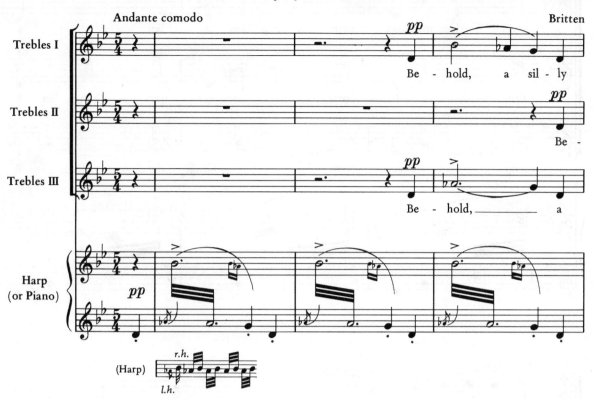

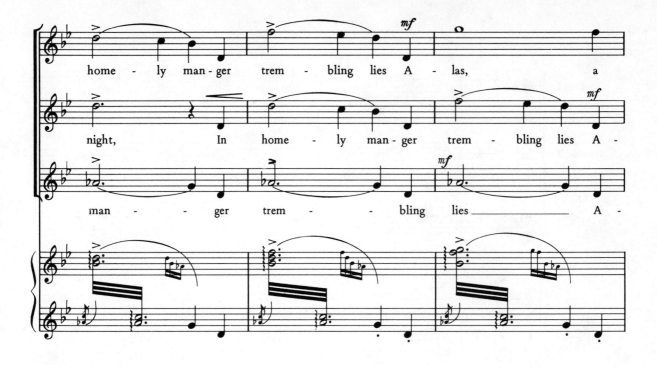

home - ly man - ger trem - bling lies A - las,   a

night,   In home - ly man - ger trem - bling lies A -

man - ger trem - bling lies _____ A -

pi - teous sight!

las,   a pi - teous sight!

las, _____ A - las, _____ a pi - teous sight!

7. Suite bergamasque: Passepied

Allegretto ma non troppo

Debussy

8. Susannah, Act II, scene 3

Andante piangendo (♪ = 96)

Susannah

Floyd

trees on the moun-tains are cold___ and bare. The sum - mer jes' va - nished an'

left ___ them there like a false - heart - ed lov - er jes' like ___ my own who

made me love_him, then left_me a - lone.

9. Five Fingers: Lento

Stravinsky

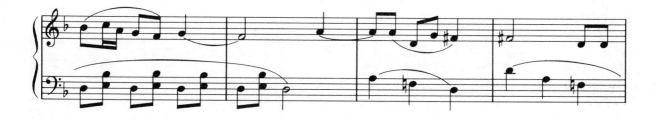

267

30
Exotic (Artificial, Synthetic) Scales

*1. Touches Noires**

Milhaud

2. Mikrokosmos, no. 78: Five Tone Scale

Bartok

3. Valsette

Kodály

4. London Symphony — Vaughn-Williams — Allegro risoluto

5. Préludes, II: Voiles* — Debussy — Modéré (♪=88) — (Dans un rythme sans rigueur et caressant.)

* Copyright 1910, Durand et Cie. Elkan-Vogel, Inc. Sole representative, United States. Used by permission of the publisher.

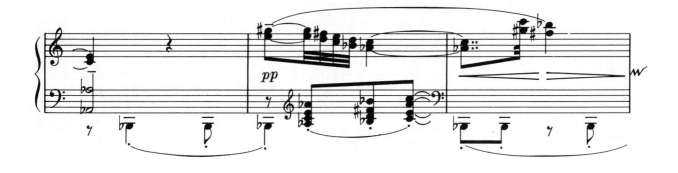

6. Mikrokosmos, no. 136: Whole Tone Scale

Andante, ♩ = 108

Bartok

7. Pelléas et Mélisande, Act II, scene I*

Lento

Debussy

* Copyright 1907, Durand et Cie. Used by permission of the publisher. Elkan-Vogel, Inc. sole representative, United States.

8. Fourteen Bagatelles, op. 6, no. 10

Bartok

Allegro (♩ = 92)

9. Bucolic, no. 2

Lutoslawski

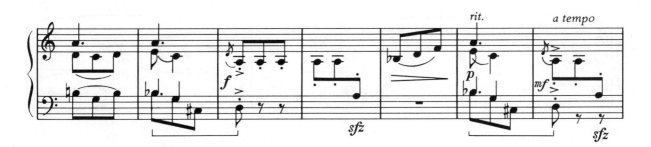

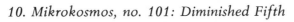

10. Mikrokosmos, no. 101: Diminished Fifth

Con moto, ♩ = 110

Bartok

11. Les Noces

tait dans sa mai - son

pei - gnait - - ses che - veux blonds fai - sait le

12. Sketches, op. 9, no. 6

Bartok

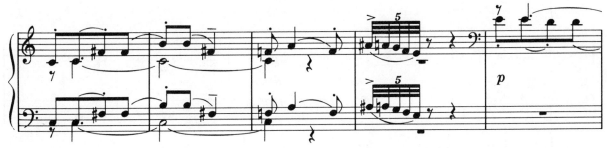

279

---

13. Fourteen Bagatelles, op. 6, no. 6

Bartok

31
Extended and Altered Tertian Harmony

1. Symphony No. 2, op. 30*

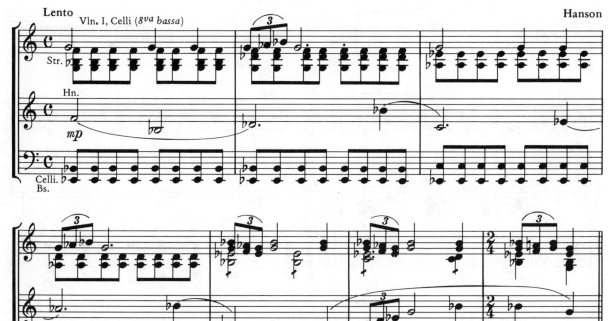

Lento   Vln. I, Celli (*8va bassa*)   Hanson

2. Four Songs, op. 2, no. 3*

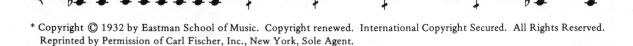

Erst ziemlich bewegt, dann langsam   Berg

Nun ich der Rie - sen Stärk - sten ü - ber - wand,

schlaf - - be - fan - gen.

---

3. Prelude, op. 34, no. 24

Allegretto

Shostakovich

4. Pelléas et Mélisande, Act I, Scene 1*

Trés modéré

Plus lent

Debussy

5. Poem, op. 31, no. 2

Allegro; con eleganza; con fiducia

Scriabin

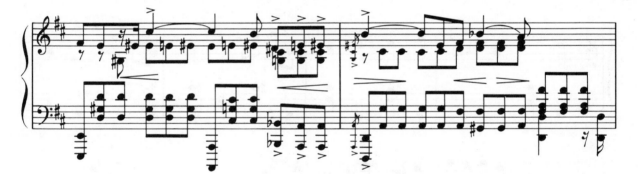

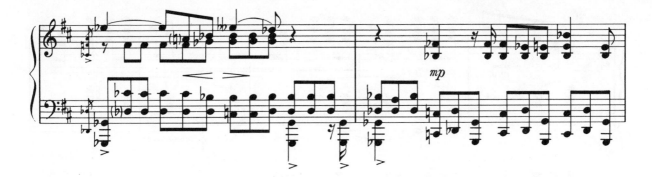

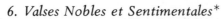

6. Valses Nobles et Sentimentales*

Modéré très franc

Ravel

* Copyright 1911, Durand et Cie. Used by permission of the publisher. Elkan-Vogel, Inc. sole representative, United States.

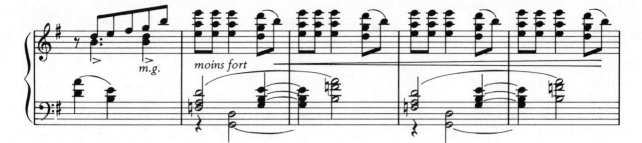

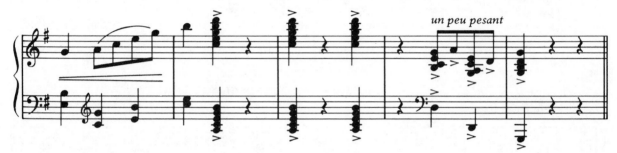

7. *Fourteen Bagatelles, op. 6, no. 4*

Bartok

8. Sonatina, op. 13

Allegro

Kabalevsky

32
Pandiatonicism
and Additive Harmony

1. Mother Goose Suite: The Magic Garden*

Ravel

2. Touches Blanches*

Milhaud

3. The Irishman Dances*

Cowell

4. The Young Pioneers*

Quite fast

Copland

5. Excursions, III

Allegretto ♩ = 60

Barber

6. Petroushka: Danse Russe

Allegro giusto ♩= 116   Stravinsky

7. Sonata for Two Pianos

Stravinsky

---

8. Gloria: Laudamus te

33
Quartal and Secundal Harmony

---

1. Mathis der Maler: Grablegung

Hindemith

---

2. A Three-Score Set, I

Schuman

3. Piano Piece, op. 39, no. 5*

Krenek

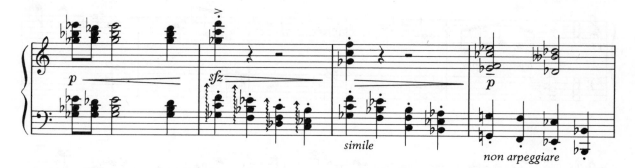

* Used by permission of Universal Edition.

4. Ludus Tonalis, Fuga secunda in G

Gay (♩= ca.200)

Hindemith

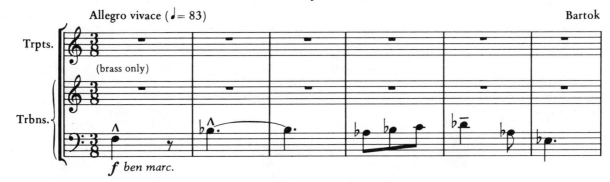

5. Concerto for Orchestra

Allegro vivace (♩= 83)

Bartok

Trpts.

(brass only)

Trbns.

f ben marc.

298

6. *Wozzeck, Act III** *

Langsam (♩.= 56-60) **aber nicht schleppen**

Berg

Marie *p*
Mä - del, was fangst Du jetzt an? _____ Hast ein klein Kind und kein

Mann! _____ Ei, was frag' ich dar - nach,

Sing' _____ ich die gan - ze Nacht.

* Used by permission of Universal Edition.

7. Mikrokosmos, no. 107: Melody in the Mist

Bartok

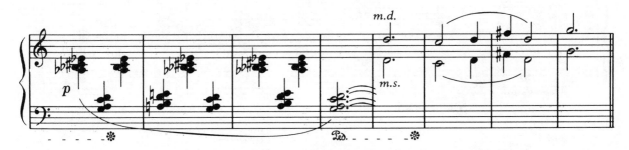

8. Wozzeck, Act II*

302

9. Tiger

Allegro feroce

Cowell

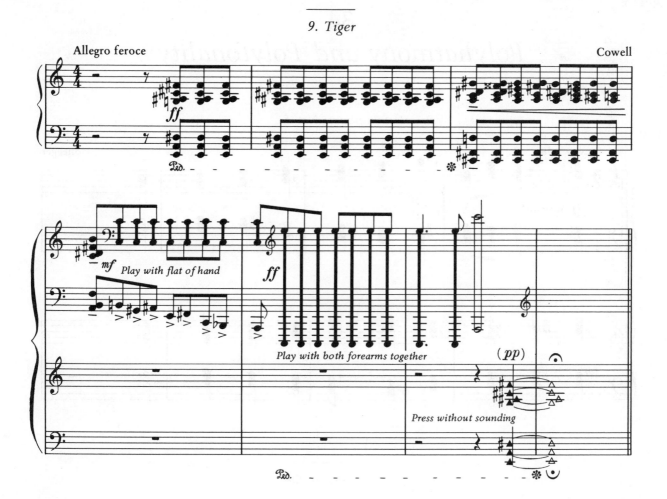

Play with flat of hand

Play with both forearms together

Press without sounding

(*pp*)

34
Polyharmony and Polytonality

1. Symphony No. 5

Honegger

2. A Three-Score Set, II

Schuman

3. Allegro Giocoso

Kraft

4. The Rake's Progress: Prelude

Stravinsky

5. Petroushka, Scene 2

Stravinsky

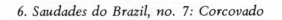

6. Saudades do Brazil, no. 7: Corcovado

Milhaud

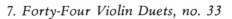

7. Forty-Four Violin Duets, no. 33

Bartok

Tempo I

35
"Interval" Music

1. Drei Klavierstücke, op. 11, no. 1

<hr/>

2. Klavierstücke, op. 19, no. 2

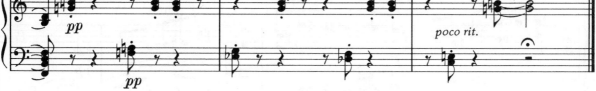

3. Klavierstücke, op. 19, no. 4

Schönberg

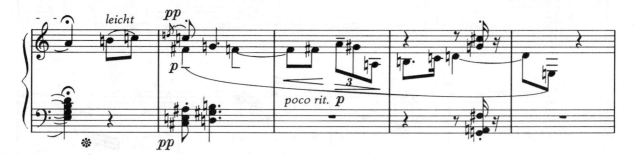

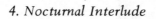

4. Nocturnal Interlude

Pisk

5. Two Episodes, I

Berger

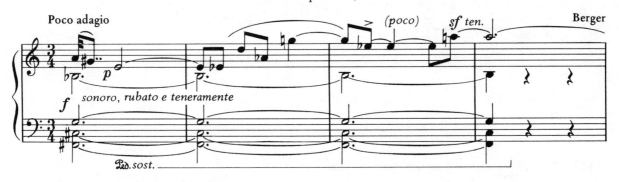

Più mosso (♩ = ca.69)

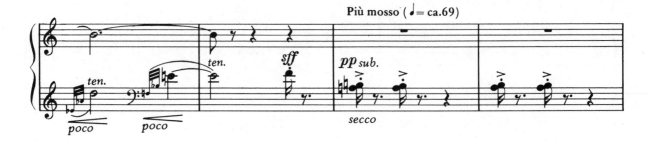

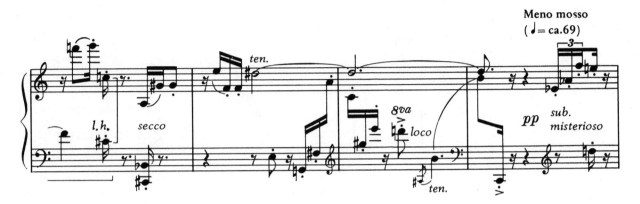

313

6. Mikrokosmos, no. 144: Minor Seconds, Major Sevenths

7. 4th String Quartet

Allegro, ♩ = 110

Bartok

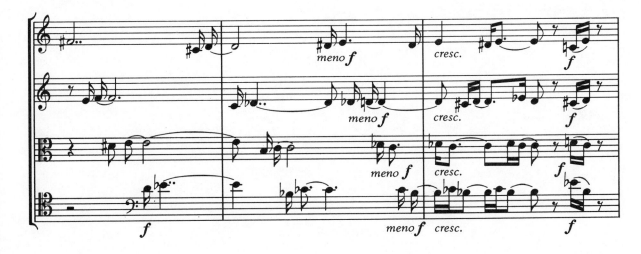

36
Twelve-Tone Serialism

1. Dancing Toys, op. 83, no. 1

Krenek

2. Duet

Babbitt

(una corda)

3. Suite für Klavier, op. 25: Gavotte*

Etwas langsam (♩ = ca.72) nicht hastig

Schönberg

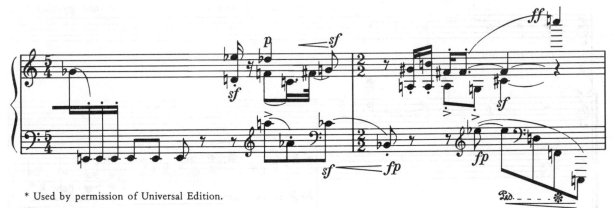

* Used by permission of Universal Edition.

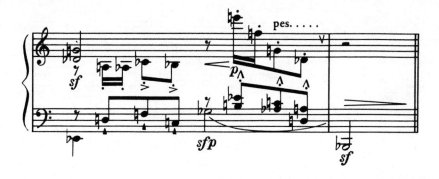

4. Cinque Frammenti di Saffo

Dallapiccola

320

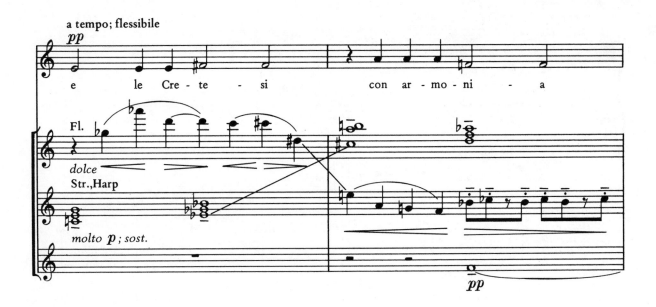

a tempo; flessibile

e le Cre - te - si   con ar - mo - ni - a

Fl.

dolce
Str.,Harp

molto *p* ; sost.

sui pie - di leg - ge - ri   co - min - cia - ro - no,

Cel.

Picc.

Ob.

Vla.

Hn.

dolce, ma in rilievo

movendo pochiss - - - -

spen - sie - ra - te, a gi - ra - re in - tor - no al -

arco

ppp Str. pizz.

Fl.

pp e appena cresc. - - - -

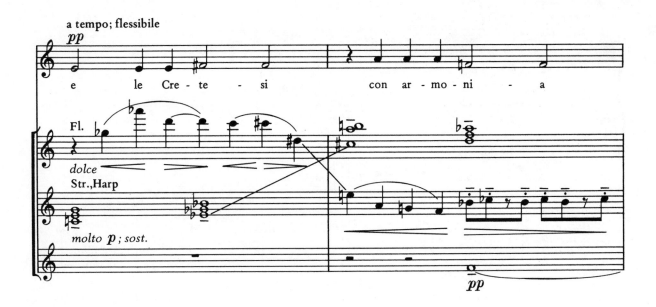

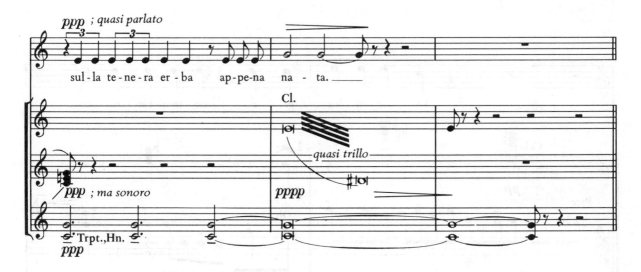

5. Drei Lieder, op. 25, no. 1*

Webern

noch ein - mal wird mir al - les grün und

leuch - tet so!   noch ü - ber -

blühn ___ die Blu - men mir die Welt! ___ noch ein -

mal ___ bin ich ganz ins Wer - den hin - ge - stellt

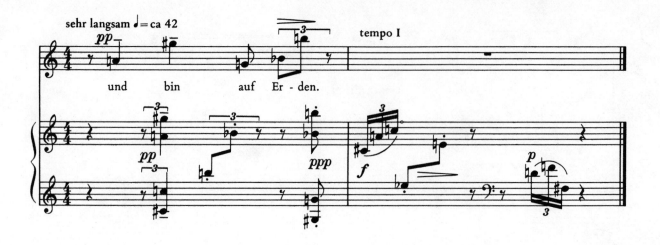

und   bin   auf   Er - den.

37
Complete Pieces for Analysis IV

1. 1ere Gymnopédie

Lent et douloureux

Satie

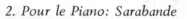

2. Pour le Piano: Sarabande

Avec une élégance grave et lente

Debussy

animez un peu

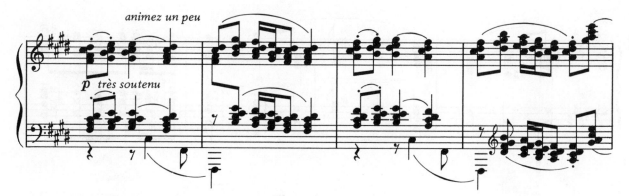

au mouvt

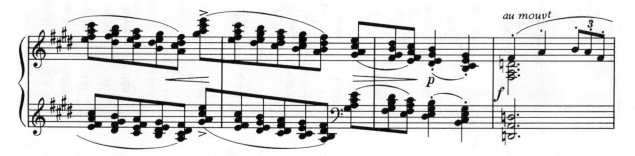

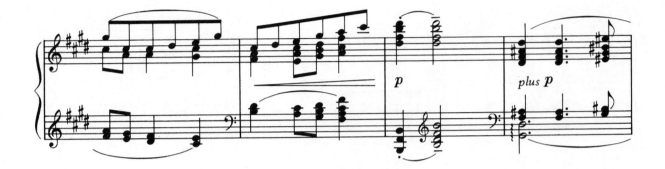

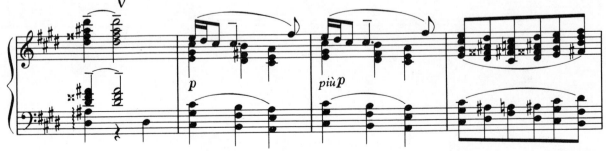

3. Préludes, X: La Cathédrale engloutie

Profondément calme (Dans une brume doucement sonore)

Debussy

(Doux et fluide)

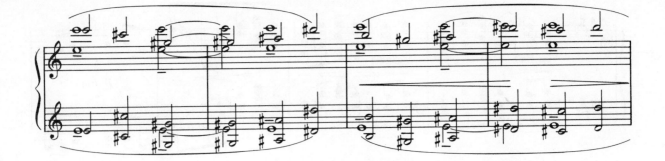

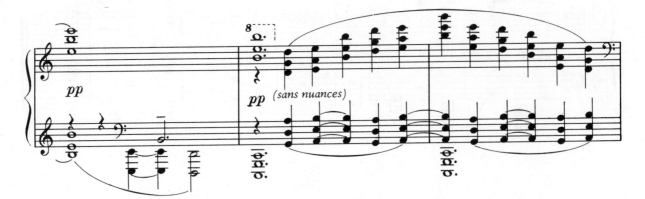

(Peu à peu sortant de la brume)

Augmentez progressivement (Sans presser)

Sonore sans dureté

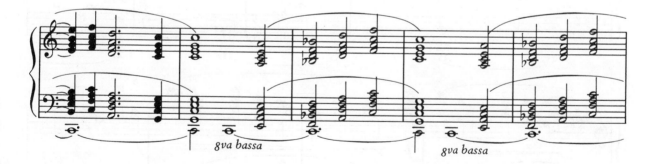

Un peu moins lent (Dans une expression allant grandissant)

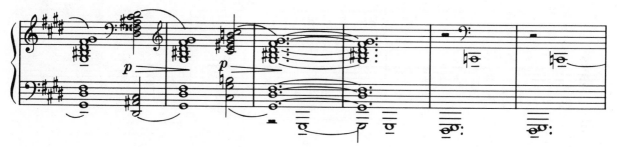

335

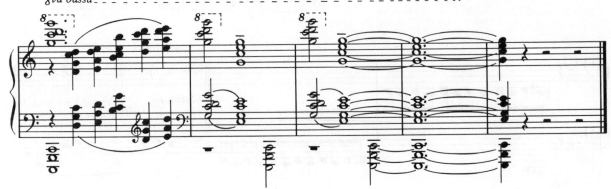

4. Sonatina

Bartok

Allegro (♩ = 140)

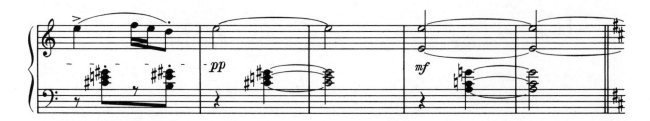

Tempo primo

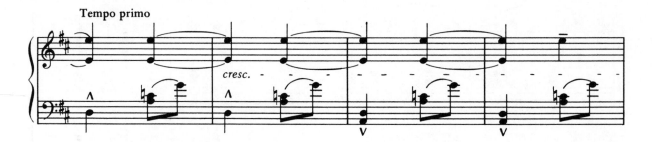

5. Classical Symphony, op. 25

Prokofiev

6. Night Song

Dello Joio

pp col pedale, molto sostenuto

342

Checklist for Analysis and Sample Analysis

All music should be analyzed as fully as possible within the limits of the student's knowledge at any stage of learning. Not only the individual elements but also their interactions should be studied. Following is a checklist of elements that should be included in an analysis.

I.   Harmonic language.
  A. All keys and chords, with Roman numerals and figured bass symbols, or appropriate contemporary nomenclature. How are the key and mode established?
  B. All modulations, indicating type and placement.
  C. All cadences, indicating type and placement.
  D. All nonharmonic tones, by type.
  E. Functional and nonfunctional use of chromaticism.
  F. Use of nonfunctional (linear, coloristic) chords.

II. Large and small formal units.
  A. Phrases and periods, if any; phrase-groups; extensions and elisions.
  B. Overall form, including large letters for main sections and formal label if appropriate. Note balance and proportion of sections.
  C. Use of repetition, altered repetition, departure, return, altered return, development, and contrast. Note use of developmental devices.
  D. Elements of unity versus elements of variety.
  E. Stable versus unstable areas (tension versus relaxation).

III. Melodic organization.
  A. Motivic structure, both melodic and rhythmic.
  B. Melodic structure, including departure note and goal note, contour, climax, main structural pitches, range, and tessitura.
  C. Special aspects, such as contrapuntal devices and sequence.

IV. Rhythmic organization.
  A. Surface rhythm, meter, harmonic rhythm.
  B. Special devices of rhythmic development.
  C. How is the meter emphasized or obscured?
  D. Tempo.

V. Sound.
    A. Use of the medium: idiomatic devices, range and tessitura,
       timbre (color).
    B. Texture.
    C. Dynamics.
VI. Text setting, where appropriate.
    A. Relations between form and/or mood of text and music.
    B. Rhythmic and/or metric relationships.

ADDITIONAL QUESTIONS, FOR THE ANALYSIS
OF TWENTIETH-CENTURY MUSIC

I.   Tonal centers, if any.
     A. How are they established?
     B. Do they change?
II. Scalar materials.
     A. What type or types are employed?
     B. Do they change or are they inflected?
III. Harmonic vocabulary.
     A. What types of chord structures are used?
     B. Is chord succession systematic? If so, how?
IV. Special metric and rhythmic characteristics.

SAMPLE ANALYSIS
Dance

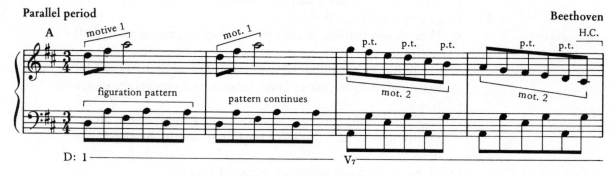

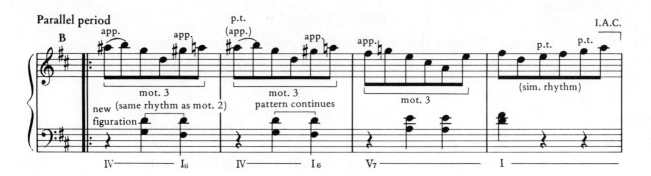

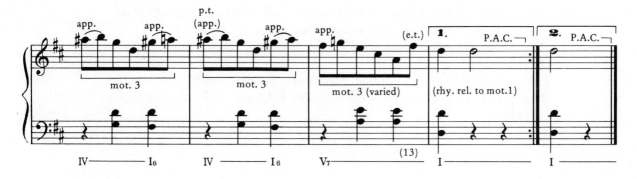

Observations

A. Form: simple binary. ‖:A:‖:B:‖

B. Each section is a parallel period consisting of two four-measure phrases.

C. There is new motivic material and a new figuration in the B section.

D. Harmonic rhythm

1. A section: slow

   𝅗𝅥. ___ | 𝅗𝅥. for first six measures.

   𝅗𝅥. for last two measures.

2. B section: faster, slowing at the cadence

   𝅗𝅥   𝅘𝅥 | 𝅗𝅥   𝅘𝅥 | 𝅗𝅥. | 𝅗𝅥. each phrase.

E. Background rhythm: eighth note motion throughout, passing from the accompanimental figuration in the A section to the melodic material in the B section and coming to rest in the final measure.

F. Melodic structure.

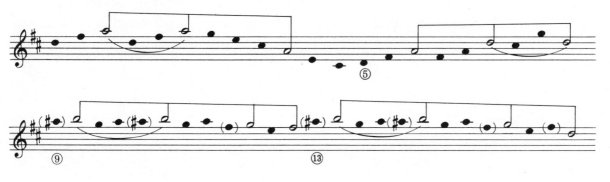

Benjamin, Thomas; Horvit, Michael; and Nelson, Robert. *Techniques and Materials of Tonal Music.* Boston: Houghton Mifflin, 1975.

Benward, Bruce. *Music in Theory and Practice.* Dubuque, Iowa: William C. Brown, 1977.

Christ, William; DeLone, Richard; Kliewer, Vernon; Rowell, Lewis; and Thomson, William. *Materials and Structure of Music.* Englewood Cliffs, N.J.: Prentice-Hall, 1966.

Dallin, Leon. *Twentieth Century Composition.* 3rd ed. Dubuque, Iowa: William C. Brown, 1974.

Forte, Allen. *Tonal Harmony in Concept and Practice.* 2nd ed. New York: Holt, Rinehart & Winston, 1962.

Persichetti, Vincent. *Twentieth-Century Harmony.* New York: Norton, 1961.

Piston, Walter. *Harmony.* 3rd ed. New York: Norton, 1962.

Siegmeister, Elie. *Harmony and Melody.* Belmont, Cal.: Wadsworth, 1966.

APPENDIX B
Translations of
Foreign Language Texts

CHAPTER 3

3. Schubert, *Wiegenlied*, op. 98, no. 2

Sleep, sleep, dear sweet child; thy Mother's hand gently rocks thee.

4. Verdi, *Rigoletto*, Act I, no. 2

This one or that one, it's all the same to me. As to the others I see around me, I don't yield my heart more to one beauty than to another.

CHAPTER 4

5. Verdi, *Rigoletto*, Act II, no. 7

Gilda: What sadness! what sadness! have rung such bitter tears.
Rigoletto: You alone remain in misery . . .

CHAPTER 5

3. Donizetti, *Lucia di Lammermoor*, Act II, no. 6

Lucy: I am so wretched that death is a blessing for me, yes, death is a blessing for
  me.
Henry: That bloody axe will always be before you.

CHAPTER 6

2. Mozart, *Bastien und Bastienne*, K. 46B, no. 9

Go on! You're telling me a fib. Bastienne, don't deceive me.

5. Mozart, *Abendempfindung*, K. 523

It's evening. The sun has faded.

CHAPTER 7

4. Mozart, *Die Zauberflöte*, K. 620, Act II, no. 21

Ring, little bells, ring. Bring my maiden here.

6. Verdi, *Rigoletto*, Act III, no. 14

Yes, revenge, terrible revenge, is this soul's only desire.

CHAPTER 8

3. Paisiello, *Le donne sur balcone*

The ladies on the balcony I know well how to evaluate,
The young men on the corner I know better how to tease.

CHAPTER 9

14. Gounod, *Faust*, Act I, no. 6

Like the gentle breeze . . .

CHAPTER 10

4. Mozart, *Bastien und Bastienne*, K. 46B, no. 1

My dear friend has forsaken me, sleep and rest have left with him.

14. Tessier, *Au joli bois je m'en vais*

To the pretty woods I go.

15. Strauss, *Der Rosenkavalier*, Act III

Sophie: It is a dream, it can't really be true that we two are together for all time
  and eternity.
Octavian: Know that I love only you and that we two are together. Everything
  passes before my sight as a dream.

20. Schubert, *Im Abendroth* (Posthumous)

O, how beautiful is Thy world, Father, when it shines like gold, when Thy
brightness falls upon it and paints the dust with shimmering brightness.

CHAPTER 12

8. Verdi, *La Traviata*, Act I, no. 2

Love, which is the moving force of the entire universe,
The mysterious one, the proud one, the cross and delight to the heart.

9. Donizetti, *Linda di Chamounix*, "O Luce di quest 'anima"

Oh, light of this soul, delight and love and life, our fate will be united on earth and
in heaven.

12. Schubert, *Aufenthalt*

Rushing stream, blustering wood, immobile rocks, my abode.

13. Schubert, *Der Wanderer*

Where are you, my beloved country? Sought for, yearned for, and never known!

15. Verdi, *Il Trovatore*, Act II, no. 11

Azucena: Plunge this blade up to the hilt into the heart of the cruel one. Strike!
Manrico: Yes, I swear it. This blade will descend into the heart of the cruel one.

CHAPTER 14

6. Mozart, *Requiem*, K. 626, Offertorium

Lord Jesus Christ, King of Glory! Free the souls of all the faithful from death's bonds.

8. Gluck, *Orphée*, Act I, no. 1

Ah, in this dark and quiet wood, Euridice, if thy spirit hears us . . .

CHAPTER 17

13. Schumann, *Widmung*, op. 25, no. 1

Thou my soul, Thou my heart, Thou my joy, oh Thou my pain, Thou my world in which I live; Thou my Heaven, wherein I soar; so Thou my grave, in which I bury my grief forever.

19. Verdi, *Rigoletto*, Act II, no. 7

In heaven, close to God, a protective angel watches. Ah, watch over this flower.

24. Schubert, *Mass in E♭ major*, Benedictus

Blessed is he who cometh in the name of the Lord.

26. Verdi, *Rigoletto*, Act II, no. 14

Pardon will come to us from Heaven. This clown knows how to strike you down.

CHAPTER 18

15. Donizetti, *Lucia di Lammermoor*, Act I

Reigning in the silence was the darkening night. The forehead was struck by a pallid ray of the gloomy moon.

20. Bononcini, *Deh più a me non vàscondete*

By unveiling yourselves (if you are about to do that) you can take this soul out of pain.

24. Bizet, *Carmen*, Act I, no. 7

My mother, I see her! Yes, I see my village again. All memories of other times! Sweet memories of the country!

CHAPTER 19

7. Schumann, *Schneeglöckchen*, op. 79, no. 29

The snow, which fell from heaven yesterday, hangs today in icicles like little bells on the slender boughs. Little snow bells ringing, what is happening in the quiet grove? Come quickly! In the grove, they're ringing in the Spring. Oh come, thou leaves, sap, and blossoms, who have been dreaming, all to Spring's shrine, come unfettered.

CHAPTER 20

8. Gounod, *Faust*, Act V, no. 18

Faust: Sweet nectar, let my heart be enshrouded in your rapture, while a kiss of fire caresses my pale brow until daybreak.

12. Bellini, *I Puritani*, Act II

Here his sweet voice was calling for me and then it disappeared. Here he was swearing to be faithful, and then the cruel one escaped from me.

14. Brahms, *Liebeslieder Walzer*, op. 52, no. 4

I wish to glow to you like the beautiful red of the evening, to please one person, to spread delight without end.

CHAPTER 21

2. Schubert, *Der Müller und der Bach*

Where a true heart pines away for love, there droop the lilies on every bank. Clouds, conceal the moon so that men may not see her tears. Angels close their eyes, and cry and sing the soul to rest.

5. Verdi, *Il Trovatore*, Act II, no. 8

Sinister shines on the terrible faces the gloomy flame that rises to the sky.

9. Brahms, *Wie Melodien zieht es mir*, op. 105

As melodies drift lightly through my senses, as spring flowers bloom and their fragrance floats away.

11. Schubert, *Mass in E♭*, Credo

I believe in one God, maker of heaven and earth.

CHAPTER 22

12. Strauss, *Der Rosenkavalier*, Act I

Having armed my heart with vigor against love, I rebelled. But I was defeated in a flash, alas! by looking at two delicate rays.

14. Schubert, *Mass in G major*, Kyrie

Christ, have mercy upon us.

20. Schumann, *Dichterliebe*, op. 48, no. 12, "Am leuchtenden Sommermorgen"

On a brightening summer morning, I go into the garden. The flowers whisper and speak, but I wander silently.

CHAPTER 23

5. Gluck, *Orphée*, Act I, nos. 6 and 7

Object of my love . . .

CHAPTER 24

8. Schubert, *Mass in G,* Benedictus

Blessed is he who cometh in the name of the Lord.

9. Schubert, *Die Allmacht,* op. 79, no. 2

Great is Jehovah the Lord, for heaven and earth proclaim His power.

CHAPTER 25

1. Schubert, *Mass in G,* Agnus Dei

Soprano: Lord God, Lamb of God.
Bass: Son of God, who taketh away the sins of the world.
Chorus: Have mercy upon us.

2. Brahms, *Wenn du nur zuweilen lächelst,* op. 57, no. 2

If you would only occasionally smile, or occasionally cool my boundless ardor . . .

5. Mozart, *Die Entführung aus dem Serail,* K. 384, Act III, no. 18

In Moorishland, a pretty maiden with black hair was imprisoned. She wept day
and night and would gladly have been rescued.

13. Brahms, *Wie bist du meine Königen,* op. 32, no. 9

Through dead wastes I wander, green shadows broadening about me, endlessly
onward through the frightful oppressiveness, pleasureful . . .

14. Schubert, *Mass in A♭,* Agnus Dei

Lamb of God, who taketh away the sins of the world, have mercy upon us.

CHAPTER 26

5. Schumann, *Waldesgespräch,* op. 39, no. 3

It is late, it is cold, why do you ride alone through the woods? The way is long, you
are alone — lovely bride, I will lead you home.

13. Fauré, *Après un Rêve*

You called me and I left the earth to fly with you toward the light. The skies half
opened their clouds to us, partially revealing unknown splendors, divine lights . . .

CHAPTER 27

2. Brahms, *Der Tod,* "Das ist die kühle Nacht," op. 96, no. 1

Death, it is the cool night; life, the sultry day.
It grows dark, I become sleepy; the day has made me tired.

CHAPTER 28

6. Schumann, *Die Lotosblume,* op. 25, no. 7

The lotus blossom fears the sun's brilliance, and with bowed head dreamily
awaits the night. The moon, her sweetheart, wakes her with his light, and she
cordially reveals to him her lovely visage. She blooms, and glows, and beams, and
stares silently up at the sky; she weeps and trembles with love and yearning.

9. Strauss, *Morgen,* op. 27, no. 4

And tomorrow the sun will shine again, and on the way where I am going, we, the
happy ones, will again be one in the midst of the sun-drenched earth. And toward
that far and hazy horizon, we will quietly and slowly wander. Mute, we will gaze
into each other's eyes, while on us falls the blissful silence.

4. Debussy, *Trois Chansons*, no. 1

God! He has made her attractive, gracious, good, and beautiful.

2. Berg, *Four Songs*, op. 2, no. 3

Now that I have defeated the strongest of giants, have found my way home from the darkest land on a white fairy-tale hand, the bells sound heavily and I stagger through the alleys, caught in sleep.

8. Poulenc, *Gloria*, Laudamus te

We praise thee.

6. Berg, *Wozzeck*, Act III

"Maiden, what are you doing now? You have a small child and no husband. Oh, what are you asking for?" I sing the whole night through.

8. Berg, *Wozzeck*, Act II

A hunter from the palace once rode through a green wood.

4. Dallapiccola, *Cinque Frammenti di Saffo*

Full shone the moon, when by the altar they stopped. And the Cretian woman, with music, upon light feet, began carefree to go about the altar, upon the tender young grass.

5. Webern, *Drei Lieder*, op. 25, no. 1

How happy I am! Once again everything becomes green and glowing to me! Still the flowers bloom over all my world! Once again I have been placed entirely in becoming and am on the earth.

APPENDIX C
Textbook Correlation Chart

CHAPTER	BENJAMIN	CHRIST	FORTE	OTTMAN	PISTON	SIEGMEISTER
1	II:2	I:17	2	I:3,6	2,3	I:2
2	II:3	I:17	2,4	I:8,10	2,3	I:3
3	II:4	I:17	5	I:19	13,18	I:14
4	II:5,6	I:17	2,4	I:8,10	2,3	I:5
5	II:8	I:19	11	I:11	9	I:11
6	II:9	I:17	3,4	I:11	5	I:10
7	II:10	I:20	2,3,4	I:14,15	2,3	I:8,10,13
8	II:11	I:18	6	I:19	13	I:14
9	II:12	I:19	11	I:18 II:3	9	I:11
10	II:14	I:21	2,3,4	I:14,17	2,3	I:8,10
11	II:15	I:18	3,4	I:14	2,3,5	I:13
12	II:16	I:22	16	I:18 II:3,7	4,12	I:12,13 II:10
13	II:17	II:3	5,6	I:19	20	I:17
14	II:18	II:4	5,6	II:5	16,17	I:17 II:7
15	II:19	II:3,4	5,6	II:5	10	I:17
17	III:1	I:24,25	4	I:20 II:8,9	14,15,16	II:1,7
18	III:2	I:26,27	9	I:20 II:1	12	II:2,3,4
20	III:3	II:5		II:9	22	II:7
21	III:4	II:8	11	II:10	23	II:10
22-24	III:5	II:9	11,16	II:11	24,26	II:10
25	III:6	II:8,18	16	II:13	12	II:7,11
26	III:7	II:15	11	II:12	18	II:9
27	IV:4	II:16	16		25,26	II:7,10
29	IV:6	II:18,20		II:14		I:5 II:12
30	IV:7	II:20		II:14		I:5 II:12
31	IV:4	II:16,17 18,20,22		II:12	21	II:10,12,13
32	IV:5	II:20,23		II:14		II:12,13
33	IV:8	II:20,22		II:14		II:13
34	IV:9	II:23		II:14		II:13
35	IV:10	II:22,23		II:14		II:13
36	IV:11	II:21,22		II:14		II:13

Books dealing only with twentieth-century techniques

CHAPTER	DALLIN	PERSICHETTI
29	3,7	2
30	4,6	2
31	4,6,7,8	1,3,5,11
32	6,7,8	5,10
33	4,6,8	1,4,6,7
34	6,8	7,12
35	4,6,7	1,2,8
36	14,15	12

Index of Composers

Babitt, Milton (1916–   ), 318
Bach, Johann Christoff Friederich (1732–1795), 52
Bach, Johann Sebastian (1685–1750), 24, 33, 47, 58, 61, 72, 86, 89, 114, 140, 142, 143, 144, 168, 177, 186, 227, 242, 243
Barber, Samuel (1910–   ), 290
Bartok, Béla (1887–1945), 259, 268, 271, 272, 273, 279, 280, 286, 297, 300, 308, 314, 315, 336
Beethoven, Ludwig von (1770–1827), 3, 4, 5, 8, 9, 13, 17, 20, 23, 26, 29, 30, 35, 36, 37, 38, 41, 44, 45, 51, 71, 73, 75, 76, 90, 97, 99, 100, 101, 103, 107, 108, 110, 111, 120, 131, 138, 145, 150, 156, 158, 159, 171, 173, 177, 179, 181, 182, 206, 209, 211, 218, 223, 235, 239, 344
Bellini, Vincenzo (1801–1835), 162
Berg, Alban (1885–1935), 281, 299, 301
Berger, Arthur (1912–   ), 312
Bizet, Georges (1838–1875), 77, 138
Bononcini, Giovanni (1670–1747), 133
Brahms, Johannes (1833–1897), 49, 55, 69, 71, 130, 137, 164, 170, 173, 196, 205, 214, 234, 237
Britten, Benjamin (1913–1976), 263
Buxtehude, Dietrich (1637–1707), 44
Byrd, William (1543–1623), 62

Chávez, Carlos (1899–   ), 260
Chopin, Frédéric (1810–1849), 5, 17, 21, 32, 116, 117, 123, 170, 175, 198, 224, 225, 233, 238
Copland, Aaron (1900–   ), 290
Corelli, Arcangelo (1653–1713), 50
Couperin, François (1668–1733), 6, 28
Cowell, Henry (1897–1965), 289, 303
Crüger, Johann (1598–1662), 47
Czerny, Carl (1791–1857), 3

Dallapiccola, Luigi (1904–1975), 320
Dandrieu, Jean (1682–1738), 28
Debussy, Claude (1862–1918), 262, 265, 270, 271, 284, 327, 331
Dello Joio, Norman (1913–   ), 341
Donizetti, Gaetano (1797–1848), 22, 65, 129

Fauré, Gabriel (1845–1924), 231
Floyd, Carlisle (1926–   ), 265
Franck, César (1822–1890), 222, 237

Gluck, Christoph Willibald (1714–1787), 83, 193
Gounod, Charles (1818–1893), 45, 160
Granados, Enrique (1867–1916), 190
Grieg, Edvard Haggerup (1843–1907), 73, 92, 187, 203, 229, 230, 251

Handel, George Frideric (1685–1759), 49, 58, 79, 84, 87, 88, 102, 110, 115, 149
Hanson, Howard (1896–   ), 281
Haydn, Franz Joseph (1732–1809), 3, 12, 25, 32, 33, 35, 40, 43, 59, 66, 72, 79(?), 80, 82, 98, 120, 121, 123, 127, 128, 131, 133, 153, 156, 163, 181, 210
Hindemith, Paul (1895–1963), 295, 297
Honegger, Artur (1892–1955), 304

Kabalevsky, Dmitri (1904–   ), 287
Kodály, Zoltán (1882–1967), 269
Kraft, Leo (1922–   ), 305
Krenek, Ernst (1900–   ), 296, 317
Kuhlau, Friederich (1786–1832), 36
Kuhnau, Johann (1660–1722), 7

Liszt, Franz (1811–1886), 157, 202
Lutoslawski, Witold (1913–   ), 272

MacDowell, Edward (1861–1908), 134
Mattheson, Johann (1681–1764), 63
Mendelssohn, Felix (1809–1847), 27, 86, 113, 184, 231, 246
Milhaud, Darius (1892–1974), 268, 288, 308
Mozart, Wolfgang Amadeus (1756–1791), 7, 10, 15, 24, 25, 26, 27, 30, 34, 39, 41, 43, 48, 52, 60, 63, 66, 74, 78, 81, 86, 97, 119, 122, 124, 128, 161, 166, 180, 190(?), 207, 244
Mussorgsky, Modeste (1839–1881), 192

Pachelbel, Johann (1653–1706), 61, 87
Paisiello, Giovanni (1740–1816), 33
Pisk, Paul (1893–   ), 312
Pleyel, Ignaz (1757–1831), 35(?)
Poulenc, Françis (1899–1963), 260, 293
Prokofiev, Serge (1891–1953), 339
Purcell, Henry (c.1659–1695), 139

ABCDEFGHIJ–M–798